Embrace
Evolve
Elevate

Embrace Evolve Elevate

Let it go. Let it be. Let it come.

KOBI JULIAN

ISBN:
979-8-9950093-1-3

This publication is designed to provide accurate and authoritative information with regard to the subject matter covered. It is sold with the understanding that the publisher is not engaged in rendering legal, accounting, or other professional advice. If legal advice or other expert assistance is required, the services of a competent professional should be sought. The opinions expressed by the author in this book are not endorsed by Robi Julian Inc and are the sole responsibility of the author rendering the opinion.

For more information, please write:
Visit us online at: www.RobiJulian.com
Cover Photography by Matt Quest Photography
@the.matt.request

Disclaimer

The contents of this book are based on personal experience, research, and the author's work as a coach, speaker, and wellness educator. The information provided is intended for personal growth, inspiration, and educational purposes only.

This book is not a substitute for professional medical, psychological, legal, or financial advice. Readers are encouraged to consult with licensed professionals in those areas when necessary. Every individual's healing and transformation journey is unique, and results may vary.

The author and publisher disclaim any liability arising directly or indirectly from the use or application of any content contained in this book. By reading this book and implementing any of its teachings, the reader accepts full responsibility for their choices and actions.

Embrace Evolve Elevate is written with the deepest intention of encouraging you to explore your own truth, honor your story, and move toward healing and wholeness—with courage, grace, and authenticity.

With love and integrity,
Robi Julian
Author | Speaker | Coach

Dedication

To my mum—
For every sacrifice you made,
For every silent prayer you whispered,
For every time you gave up something so
I could have more.

Your strength carried me.
Your love shaped me.
And your unwavering faith in me lit the
way when I couldn't see it myself.

Because of you, I learned how to rise.
Because of you, I found the courage to
become who I was always meant to be.
This book, this journey, and every
breakthrough within its pages—
they exist because you sacrificed so much
of yourself for my existence.

With all my love,

Your daughter, Kobi

Acknowledgments

First and foremost, I give all the glory to God—the source of all wisdom, healing, and divine timing. This book was birthed from both pain and purpose, and I am deeply grateful for the grace that carried me through every word and every season.

To my incredible publishing team—thank you for believing in my voice, my vision, and the message behind *Embrace Evolve Elevate*. Your guidance and support made this book more than a manuscript—it became a movement.

To my friends—Eliza, Piper, Ron, Kiran, Ajooni, Justin, Alexia, and Soraya. You have been my tribe, my anchor, and my light in the moments when this journey felt too heavy to carry alone. Thank you for believing in me, for cheering me on, and for holding space for my dreams. This book carries pieces of each of you—your love, your hope, your encouragement.

To my children, the truest parts of my heart:

Hannan — You are my life. Your strength, resilience, and unwavering spirit continue to inspire me every single day. Watching you become the man you are is one of my greatest joys.

Nikki — You are my love. Your tenderness, courage, and compassion reflect the very heart of this book. You remind me to lead with grace and live with intention.

Eamon — You are my light. Your laughter, your energy, and your brilliance light up my world. Thank you for reminding me to shine even when life feels dim.

This book is for anyone on the journey of becoming—of letting go, growing forward, and rising higher. But to my children, know this: you are my why.

With all my love,

Robi Julian

Author | Speaker | Coach

Advanced Praise

"For anyone looking to fulfill a greater purpose in life, *Embrace Evolve Elevate* is the book for you. Kobi's warm spirit bleeds through the pages as she offers inspiration and practical advice to grow. My soul was filled with encouragement as I felt like I had my own personal coach telling me, *You can do this!*"

— Pastor Benjamin Jones,
Lead Pastor-Reflection Church

"*Embrace Evolve Elevate* is a soul-nourishing guide that gently walks readers through the sacred work of healing, self-love, and forgiveness. Kobi Julian writes with clarity and compassion, offering wisdom that feels both practical and divinely inspired. Her personal stories and insight create a sense of connection and encouragement, especially for those newly embracing a wellness journey. Tools like the 'sandwich method' for setting boundaries are powerful yet simple ways to honor yourself with grace. This book is a beautiful invitation to grow, release, and rise into wholeness."

— Dr. Yuri Kozman, Public Health
Educator & Wellness Coach

"This book changed me. Kobi's voice is compassionate, clear, and captivating. *Embrace Evolve Elevate* isn't just inspiring—it's actionable. As a transformational life coach, author, and speaker, Kobi Julian delivers practical wisdom and heartfelt truth that stays with you long after the final page. It's one of those rare books you'll want to keep close and revisit often."

— Theresa Amrhein, coaching client

A Gift for You

As a thank you for investing in *Embrace Evolve Elevate*—and in yourself—I'd love to bless you with a special gift.

I created a free transformational resource designed to support your next steps, whether you're ready to set bold goals, deepen your self-love journey, or rediscover your purpose. It's my way of saying: you're not alone, and you're already on your way.

 Download your free gift today at:

 **www.KobiJulian.com**

This companion tool is a beautiful next step in your journey of healing, growth, and elevation. I pray it inspires you, empowers you, and keeps your fire lit.

With love and purpose,

Kobi Julian
Author | Speaker | Coach

Table of Contents

Introduction

Have you ever felt like there's more to you than what meets the eye, like a reservoir of untapped energy and hidden potential waiting to be unleashed? Many people feel this way at some point. This book explores the powerful connection between embracing your past, evolving in the present, and ultimately elevating yourself to a higher level of being. When you step fully into your best self, that's when the magic begins.

So, what truly holds people back from becoming their best selves? Fear, doubt, uncertainty, and toxic relationships are just a few of the common barriers. Many aspire to change, take bold steps, or pursue dreams—only to be met by that inner voice whispering, *"What if I fail? What if I'm not good enough? What if I don't deserve it?"* These thoughts feed a cycle of self-doubt, fear, and limiting beliefs—some of the most paralyzing emotions one can face.

People begin to compare their lives to others, measure their success by someone else's standards, and forget the uniqueness of their journey. The opinions of others start to shape their self-worth. As a result, they become entangled in a fog of negativity, self-doubt, and toxic influences. But what if there was a way to break free? What if each person held the power to overcome these obstacles and unlock their true potential?

Taking the time to understand what holds a person back—their fears, doubts, and true desires—is the essence of self-reflection. It demands complete honesty and a willingness to confront one's weaknesses to grow. True reflection involves cultivating self-awareness, self-acceptance, and self-love. Time and again, individuals who fully embrace this process have overcome immense challenges and unlocked extraordinary potential. The transformation is remarkable.

There is often a pivotal moment when everything shifts. It's the decision to stop playing small, to no longer allow fear and doubt to lead, and to begin believing in your worth. It's the realization that you are enough, that you are worthy, and that you have so much more to give. In that moment, something powerful awakens—and the magic begins to unfold.

In that moment, everything changes. The world takes on a new light. Opportunities begin to appear. Life starts to align with authenticity, rich with purpose, passion, and meaning. It becomes a life full of wonder, magic, awe, prosperity, abundance, and love. This experience is possible—and it's within reach.

Why trust the words written on the pages of this book? With two black belts in life—one in failure, one in success—alongside two master's degrees in health and education, I have a wide range of certifications in the wellness field. I also have over 16 years of experience as an educator, health coach, business owner, and mother of three. I bring both personal and professional insight. For more than a decade, I've helped individuals achieve their well-being goals, create abundance, and live fulfilled, prosperous lives. More importantly, I've walked this path myself.

Using the techniques outlined in this book, many individuals have regained their health and vitality, balanced their energy, embraced a more positive mindset, and discovered a sense of inner peace. They have rebuilt confidence, found renewed motivation, achieved financial stability, and uncovered their deeper life purpose.

But the path to this understanding hasn't always been smooth. Like many, I've faced emotional and spiritual challenges. These experiences taught me it's not about avoiding hardship—but about how I choose to respond to it. This book invites individuals on a journey of self-discovery, perseverance, and transformation.

Struggles with self-doubt, anxiety, and failure were once constant companions. At times, it felt as though these emotions might consume everything. I questioned my abilities, second-guessed decisions, and feared an uncertain future. These feelings seeped into my daily life, making it difficult to focus, to sleep, even to get out of bed. It felt like a battle I was losing.

There were times when it felt like being stuck in a rut, trapped by the belief that success and happiness was out of reach and that nothing would ever be good enough. The worst part? Not knowing how to escape it. It was like drowning in a sea of negativity with no lifeline in sight. That kind of cycle can become vicious, but breaking free from it was non-negotiable. Slowly, and with intention, progress began to take shape. No matter how hard it got, moving forward became the only option.

My shift began by focusing on my strengths instead of shortcomings. Surrounding myself with positive, encouraging people made a difference—people who believed in the possibility of change. Small, consistent actions led to meaningful strides. Emotional challenges once viewed as weaknesses began to feel like growth opportunities.

One of the most significant turning points come with the realization that emotional challenges are not unique to only a few. Many people—regardless of how successful they appear—grapple with their internal battles. This understanding is incredibly liberating. It creates a sense of belonging, a recognition that humanity is part of a broader community striving and struggling together.

The emotions that I felt for the first time I shared my story—truly opened up about my fears and doubts—was terrifying. But it was also freeing. For the first time, I felt authentic because I was finally being true to myself. That's when real growth began.

The pivotal shift happened when I stopped seeing my emotional challenges as weaknesses. Instead, they became markers of strength—proof of resilience and compassion forged through adversity. From that point forward, I began wearing my journey like a badge of honor rather than a source of shame.

Looking back, it's clear that growth isn't about perfection—it's about the willingness to learn and evolve through each experience. It's about facing fear and doubt with courage and emerging stronger on the other side. This book invites readers to find inspiration through that lens.

Throughout its chapters, readers will discover uplifting stories, practical exercises, and actionable steps designed to help them take ownership of their lives and shape a future aligned with their core values. The focus here is not on surface-level change, but on deep, internal transformation—leading to a more authentic, purpose-driven, and fulfilling life.

This is an invitation to begin a journey of self-discovery, continuous development, and the elevation of spirit and potential. The goal is to empower each reader to embrace their inner strength and confidently pursue the life they are meant to live, honoring their path with openness and resolve.

May this book serve as a beacon, guiding readers toward a future where growth, compassion, and legacy come together to shape a world filled with possibility. It is dedicated to the dreamers, the doers, and the ever-evolving souls who enrich the world every day.

Part One:
Embrace-Let it Go

Embracing one's true self is among the most powerful and liberating actions a person can take. When individuals accept and love themselves without apology or pretense, they open the door to a life filled with freedom, joy, and genuine connection. Living authentically often leads to a deeper sense of happiness and fulfillment that might otherwise remain out of reach.

My utmost desire and passion for you, as you read the pages of this book, is to offer a new way to look at the past and understand that there is hope for a fulfilled and content life when one chooses to believe in themselves and learn from the lessons of life no matter how painful they might have been.

Before you move on, take a moment to pause and breathe. The guided meditation that follows is designed to help you embody the healing from the past. Let the sound carry you deeper into your transformation—into alignment, release, and renewal. Embrace, immerse, and let it go.

CHAPTER ONE

The Purpose to My Pain

This chapter is dedicated to every soul who has felt the sting of pain, the weight of sorrow, or the crushing blow of adversity. It honors those who have stumbled and fallen—yet found the strength to rise again. It's for anyone who has stared in darkness and dared to search for light.

This is a tribute to the quiet warriors of the heart, the champions of resilience, and the silenced heroes who find purpose within their pain. It stands as a testament to the indomitable human spirit—proof that growth can bloom even in the harshest conditions.

It celebrates an unwavering belief in the transformative power of hardship, the beauty that can emerge from broken places, and the hope that flickers even in the darkest moments. For those walking through loss, fear, or uncertainty, this chapter is an acknowledgment of your strength, perseverance, and unfolding journey toward healing and meaning.

May these words offer solace, inspiration, and guidance to uncover the unique path to healing and wholeness. This is a dedication to the power of human resilience, to the beauty of the human spirit, and to the potential for growth that resides within every soul, regardless of the pain experienced. May this chapter serve as a beacon of hope, guiding individuals towards a brighter future, one where they discover not only the purpose in their pain but the profound beauty that emerges from its ashes.

My life story is a chapter marked by profound transformation. From unrest to spiritual grounding, from fleeing a homeland on the brink of war to building a new life in an unfamiliar world, it is a journey shaped by both loss and discovery—a constant dance between the two.

Born in Iran to a Muslim family immersed in traditional practices, I was raised with the same moral foundations as my peers. Yet, something stirred differently within me. The beliefs passed down through generations failed to satisfy my spiritual curiosity. I longed to explore beyond the limits of doctrine, to experience faith freely and deeply. That yearning, however, was overshadowed by a greater hardship—the kind that alters lives without warning: war.

At a very young age, everything familiar was stripped away. By the time I turned seven, a violent revolution erupted, shaking every corner of my country. Soon after, war broke out, leaving millions devastated, including my own family. I was exposed to tremendous losses and devastation as the war brutally snatched my brother, my cousins, and my neighbors, tearing holes in both my life and my community. I witnessed firsthand how war can destroy not just cities, but the very fabric of people's lives.

By thirteen, I had lost my brother, the one who had promised to return home in just a few weeks. He kept his promise but came back in a body bag. Of all my siblings, I knew he loved me the most. Still, in that moment, I felt deeply confused, betrayed, and abandoned—like love had failed to keep its word.

After that catastrophic loss, my parents made the heart-wrenching decision to send me away in search of a better life. I was among the fortunate few who found a way out of the warzone. My new home was in a different world entirely. But the road to what many called "The Land of Opportunity" was anything but smooth.

When I first moved to America, the language barrier was one of the biggest challenges. On top of that, I was alone—my parents didn't stay with me, and the loneliness was overwhelming. I had already lost my brother, and now I had to adjust to a new place, a new culture, and a new language—all without the comfort of my family. It was a time in life when parental love and guidance felt essential, yet I had to navigate it all on my own. I still hadn't fully grieved my brother's death, and my parents' absence added an even heavier weight to carry. I felt invisible, unimportant, and unloved.

Years later, as an adult, I graduated high school with honors and earned two master's degrees—all while raising children who became the joy, love, and light of my life. Still, something inside me felt unsettled, like a vital piece of the puzzle was missing.

For a long time, it felt like life was on autopilot—moving forward without direction or purpose. Each day blurred into the next, filled with tasks that seemed important on the surface but left a lingering sense of restlessness underneath. The actions followed expectations, yet fulfillment remained out of reach. That nagging question echoed often: *Is this all there is to life?* It wasn't living—it was merely existing.

In an attempt to fill the growing void, distractions became the norm. Fleeting pleasures, temporary highs—not substances, but expensive purchases and surface-level achievements—offered momentary relief. I surrounded myself with things that looked valuable but added nothing to who I truly was. Despite the effort, the emptiness persisted. Life felt like a waking dream, one where purpose was elusive and meaning distant.

I would often feel like I was stuck in a rut, like I was just repeating the same patterns over and over again, without any real sense of progress or growth. It was a frustrating and demotivating place to be, and I didn't know how to get out of it. I was just going through life without any real sense of passion or purpose.

But then something started to shift inside of me. I started to tune into my intuition, to listen to my own heart and desires. I started to ask myself some really tough questions: (1) what truly makes me happy, (2) what gets me excited, and (3) what I'm passionate about. And slowly but surely, I started to uncover clues that would eventually lead me to my purpose in life.

It wasn't easy. There were countless moments of doubt—times when giving up felt like the only option. Unpleasant emotions surfaced, overwhelming and unfamiliar. Progress often seemed fleeting: two steps forward, three steps back. But my journey didn't stop there. I kept pushing forward, kept seeking, kept searching. And then, one day, it hit me.

With persistence came clarity. What if my focus shifted to strengths instead of weaknesses? What if my environment included people who encouraged, supported, and believed in me? Small steps began to replace hesitation—steps that grew into leaps. Emotional challenges, once viewed as flaws, gradually revealed themselves as catalysts for growth.

The first time I shared my story—the first admitting to my fear and doubt—was terrifying. But it was also liberating. That moment of vulnerability marked the beginning of something deeper: authenticity. And that's when real growth began.

The pivotal moment for me came when I realized that my emotional challenges were not something to be ashamed of, but rather something to be proud of. I realized that my struggles had made me stronger, more resilient, and more compassionate, and that's when everything changed for me. That's when I started to see my emotional journey as a badge of honor, rather than a source of shame.

There was a moment of clarity—a profound understanding of purpose. It felt as though the Universe opened up. The path became clear: to share my story honestly, embracing both the tears and the triumphs. In that instant, every struggle, setback, and challenge finally made sense.

There were times marked by sorrow, anger, and resentment. Love felt scarce, and bitterness took root. But over time, that pain revealed itself as part of a greater purpose—a journey of transformation. This book shares that journey. To reconnect with a clearer, stronger, more luminous version of myself, it became necessary to remove the layers of shame, guilt, failure, and other emotional burdens that once defined my environment and identity.

This path wasn't about perfection. It was about the willingness to face fears, confront doubts, and grow through every experience. I hope that my story can inspire others to do the same.

Past experiences—mistakes, losses, adventures, and painful lessons—shaped the person I've become. Without them, I wouldn't be here. Embracing those events, rather than resisting them, was key. Shifting perspective from bitterness to acceptance turned out to be essential in building a life grounded in peace and purpose.

According to various studies, only around 25% of Americans report having a clear sense of purpose in life. This suggests that a significant portion of the population may feel as though they are moving through life without clear direction. A strong sense of purpose has the power to transform lives. It brings clarity—an inner knowing of why one does what they do and how each action leads toward something meaningful. When individuals live in alignment with their purpose, they often experience a deeper sense of fulfillment and joy than they previously believed possible.

5 Life-Changing Tips for Finding Purpose

Uncovering one's true purpose is one of the most impactful steps a person can take toward lasting fulfillment. A clear purpose brings direction, focus, and motivation. It serves as a personal roadmap, guiding decisions that reflect one's deepest values and passions.

Yet, many struggle with this discovery. It's common to feel stuck in a routine, merely going through the motions of daily life without meaning or direction. Societal expectations often add pressure, pushing individuals to follow conventional paths instead of pursuing authentic dreams. Some may even believe they are too young, too old, or simply not enough to make a meaningful change.

One of the greatest barriers to self-realization is the fear of what might surface. What if I'm not good enough? What if the life I've been living isn't aligned with who I truly am? These questions can be unsettling—no wonder self-reflection is often delayed. Yet, growth begins when individuals choose to face these fears directly. It's through honest confrontation of the hidden or avoided parts of the self that transformation becomes possible.

The fear of failure can be paralyzing. It often holds people back from taking risks or exploring new possibilities. To feel secure, many seek validation from others, molding themselves to fit expectations rather than carving out their unique path. The uncertainty of change can also be intimidating, making familiarity—even if unfulfilling—feel like the safer choice.

Fear and doubt often cloud inner wisdom, leaving individuals feeling stuck in a cycle of busyness without progress. It can feel like running on a hamster wheel—constant motion, but no forward movement. But imagine what could happen if those limiting beliefs were dismantled. Imagine tapping into untapped potential, discovering passions and desires that could serve as a compass toward a more meaningful, authentic life.

1. Turning Weakness into Strength-Conquering Struggles and Overcoming Adversity

Understanding one's strengths and weaknesses is a vital step in personal growth. Instead of dwelling on shortcomings, individuals are encouraged to identify their core strengths and explore how these abilities can be used to make a meaningful impact. The kind of impact that brings fulfillment and a sense of purpose, enough to inspire a person to rise each day with energy and intention. Creating change doesn't always require grand gestures; it often stems from small, consistent choices that shape a more positive life and world.

Transforming weaknesses into strengths is a powerful skill that contributes significantly to long-term success. This process involves channeling life's greatest challenges as fuel for forward momentum, rather than allowing them to become barriers. Like any other ability, it can be cultivated over time through patience, persistence, and intentional practice.

Struggles are not weaknesses—they are strengths in disguise. Often, it's the deepest challenges that shape the greatest triumphs. Reframing difficulties as growth opportunities is not just inspiring—it's essential. This mindset shift is key to unlocking true potential and moving closer to the life envisioned. Facing fear and embracing adversity with purpose opens doors to resilience, growth, and success.

2. Unlock True Passion-Turn Hobbies into Success

Exploring true passions begins with asking: What brings genuine joy during free time? What topics spark curiosity and enthusiasm? Imagine waking up each morning, excited to engage in work that feels meaningful. That's the result of transforming hobbies into purposeful ventures. These efforts not only offer personal fulfillment but can also lead to financial success and a deep sense of accomplishment.

Once clear about one's strengths and value, the next step is connection. Attend networking events, participate in online forums, and engage with those already doing the work envisioned. While networking may feel daunting, it is a critical bridge between passion and purpose-driven success. By living out core values and generously sharing knowledge and skills, passion becomes more than a pastime—it becomes a way of life.

3. Core Values-What Really Matters

Values are the compass by which individuals navigate life. What truly matters? What types of relationships foster growth? What kind of person does one aspire to be? Understanding core values is essential for personal development and effective decision-making. These values serve as guiding principles, shaping behavior, relationships, and actions. They are the foundation on which a meaningful and purpose-driven life is built, with lasting effects on well-being and fulfillment.

Living in alignment with personal values often results in greater confidence, authenticity, and satisfaction. It creates a sense of ownership over one's life, rather than the feeling of merely going through the motions. This alignment strengthens one's connection with both self and others, cultivating a deeper peace with the world.

Clarity about core values enhances decision-making and inspires action. When individuals understand what matters most to them, they are more likely to pursue challenges, step outside their comfort zones, and live with intention. Rather than settling for "good enough," they aim for truly meaningful lives.

As core values become clearer, patterns begin to emerge. Priorities sharpen, and distractions fade. Choices start reflecting deeper convictions rather than external expectations—and that's when transformation begins.

4. Stepping Out of The Comfort Zone

Growth requires stepping into unfamiliar territory and embracing calculated risks. While it may feel intimidating, venturing outside of one's comfort zone is often the catalyst for personal transformation. Consider this: When was the last time something new sparked excitement or discomfort? How often are opportunities missed simply because they lie on the other side of fear?

Comfort zones provide routine and safety, but rarely growth. Repeating the same actions daily may feel easy, but it limits potential. Without discomfort, there's no push to improve, no reason to evolve, and no chance to experience more. Take a moment to reflect! What possibilities are slipping away due to hesitation? What breakthroughs remain unexplored because of a reluctance to leap?

Trying new things can profoundly shape a person's life. Stepping out of one's comfort zone opens the door to new experiences, fresh perspectives, and unexpected growth. It builds confidence, presents new challenges, and fosters personal development. Suddenly, the world looks different— and so does the person in the mirror. With each step into the unknown, individuals often discover they're capable of far more than they believed. That realization is deeply empowering.

Consider this: When was the last time you tried something new or challenged yourself to break routine? Was it a positive experience? Did you uncover something unexpected about yourself? Often, those who consistently embrace new challenges find themselves growing in confidence and uncovering fresh opportunities.

One of the most significant changes I experienced after stepping out of my comfort zone was when I decided to start my own business. It was a huge risk, but it was also an incredible opportunity for growth. I had to learn new skills, I had to adapt to new situations, and I had to push myself to be better every single day. It wasn't easy, but it was worth it. I learned so much about myself and the new business. The outcome was that I learned about perseverance. It changed me. It changed the way I approach challenges; it changed the way I take calculated risks, and it created a new way I approach life.

The takeaway? Growth begins at the edge of discomfort. Challenge yourself. Take the risk. See what unfolds.

5. Trust The Gut- Following Intuition Can Change Life

Intuition is a powerful internal compass. It's that quiet voice nudging individuals toward their deeper purpose—a subtle awareness that often knows what's right or wrong long before the conscious mind can explain why. Though sometimes dismissed as just a "gut feeling," intuition plays a vital role in everyday decision-making.

Many have been conditioned to view intuition as unreliable and it's nothing more than a gut feeling or a hunch, favoring logic and reason over instinct. This mindset, however, can lead to chronic overthinking, self-doubt, and even paralysis by analysis. When intuition is ignored, so is a key part of the decision-making process. The subconscious mind—capable of processing information rapidly and intuitively—is left untapped, despite its remarkable ability to process vast amounts of information far more efficiently than the conscious mind.

Intuition is a powerful tool that has often been unfairly dismissed. When embraced rather than ignored, it allows access to the subconscious mind, leading to more informed and confident decisions, therefore, trusting that gut feeling can reveal its true value. Psychological research confirms that intuition is a real cognitive process—one in which the brain draws from past experiences, internal signals, and environmental cues to make decisions. These decisions often occur so rapidly that they bypass conscious awareness.

Discovering one's true purpose can feel like shedding a heavy burden. In my own experience, it brought a clarity and direction I had never known. By following the steps outlined earlier, I began to prioritize my strengths over my weaknesses. My passion, fueled by a deep desire, aligned with my core values as I stepped outside my comfort zone. And it all began when I chose to trust my intuition.

My purpose became clear: to help others by making a positive impact through telling my story and shared experiences. That purpose was forged through personal pain: (1) the loss of my brother, (2) the abandonment by my parents, and (3) the belief that I was unlovable.

Opening up and allowing myself to be vulnerable wasn't easy, but the journey has been transformative. That same sense of purpose and fulfillment is possible for everyone. A life aligned with one's true self is not only achievable—it's deeply rewarding.

Before you turn the page, I invite you to breathe deeply and gently step into the meditation that follows. Let it hold space for your pain, your power, and the quiet transformation that is already unfolding within you.

CHAPTER TWO

The Blame Game

This chapter is dedicated to the countless individuals who have endured hardship and adversity yet found the strength within themselves to rise above the limitations of victimhood. It is dedicated to those who have bravely confronted their past traumas and chosen to build resilient and fulfilling lives. It is a testament to the human spirit's capacity for healing, growth, and profound transformation.

This chapter is for those who have felt the crushing weight of blame (blaming others and blaming oneself), who have struggled to understand their experiences, and who yearn to reclaim their personal power. May these pages offer solace, understanding, and a pathway toward a life defined by empowerment and lasting peace.

There are certainly bad people in this world. There are corrupt governments. There are individuals who mistreat and abuse others—and they will ultimately be held accountable. However, the way one responses to such actions is entirely the individual's responsibility. Embracing this truth, even in situations involving significant mistreatment, is a powerful step toward healing and growth.

This is a journey of reclaiming personal power and building a life defined not by blame, but by strength, resilience, and lasting peace. By understanding the root causes of blame, developing emotional regulation skills, and cultivating resilience, individuals can regain control of their lives and create a brighter future.

Although blaming others may offer temporary relief—a misguided effort to restore control in the midst of chaos—the long-term consequences are often harmful, affecting nearly every aspect of life.

By consistently placing blame on external factors, individuals relinquish their power to influence their own lives. This mindset undermines motivation to seek solutions, learn from mistakes, or develop effective coping mechanisms. Instead, it fosters a reactive state—one in which people passively accept whatever life presents.

Avoiding personal responsibility comes at a significant cost. Externalizing blame transfers control to circumstances and others, diminishing one's ability to respond proactively to challenges. Rather than becoming problem-solvers, individuals risk becoming passive recipients of events, often caught in a cycle of resentment and helplessness.

Over time, this erodes self-efficacy, leading to deep frustration, persistent anger, and resentment toward those perceived as responsible. Such emotional burdens can be crippling, impacting personal relationships, limiting professional growth, and compromising overall well-being.

Who's Really to Blame?

We've all been there—pointing fingers at our moms for everything that's gone wrong in life. It's easy. They've always been present with advice, guidance, love—and yes, sometimes, criticism and judgment. But the truth is, mothers often play a significant role in shaping who we become.

It's tempting to say, "Mom, this is your fault." When one is running late: *"Why didn't you wake me up on time?"* Or fumbling through a recipe: *"Why didn't you teach me how to cook? I lived off ramen noodles for years!"* And when the pressure of life becomes too much: *"Why didn't you show me how to set boundaries or say no?"* These thoughts come easily, but the reality behind them is more complex.

However, my situation was different. I didn't have my mother beside me during my teenage years—those critical moments when her presence would have mattered most. I couldn't blame her for everything that went wrong, like missing school, struggling with cooking, or always being late. But I blamed her for everything else that I did not want to take responsibility for.

As mentioned in the previous chapter, I fled the country where I was born. Much of my childhood was shaped by forces beyond my control—my birthplace, the culture I grew up in, the war. I wasn't alone in facing such catastrophic hardship. What later became empowering, both as an adult and as a mother, was understanding the deeper reasons behind it all.

My mother did the best she could with what she had. She made sure I had a safe environment to grow into the person I am today. But at thirteen, I couldn't understand or accept any of that. The war that destroyed my country and claimed countless lives—including my 22-year young brother—is something I may never fully comprehend. And at that young age, I certainly couldn't grasp why my parents sent me to the United States. It was a decision made of love and a desire to protect me. However, back then, it didn't feel that way.

My brother sacrificed his life for my freedom? Why? None of it made sense to me. From a child's perspective, it felt like no one loved me. My brother was gone—no longer there to protect me—and my parents had seemingly abandoned me. Losing someone I loved and being sent away didn't feel like love. Where was the love I so desperately needed? Where could I find it? Did I even deserve it?

The answers to those self-destructive questions only became clear after the loss of my mother—a loss that reshaped my soul. A mother's love is one of the most powerful forces in the world: unrelenting, unconditional, unwavering. From the moment a child is born, her love guides, supports, and nurtures. As the child grows, that love deepens, molding them into who they are meant to become.

Being a mother is a challenging job, to say the least. It requires patience, understanding, and a willingness to put someone else's needs before her own. And yet, mothers do it all with a smile, often sacrificing their own well-being and happiness for the sake of their family. That was my mom. She sacrificed herself and sent me to the other side of the world so I can survive, so I can have a life, so I can be a mother one day, so I can do the same sacrifice for my own children. She gave me life at the expense of her broken heart.

But as much as mothers give, they also face their own unique set of challenges. They deal with the pressure of being perfect—of being everything to everyone, all the time. They navigate the complex web of parenting, often without a roadmap or a guide. And they do it all while holding onto their identities, their hopes, and their dreams. It's a difficult tightrope to walk, yet mothers do it every day with grace and courage.

I saw my mom losing her identity to raise her children. She lost a son when she was in her late thirties and carried that grief for as long as I can remember. She managed to send me to a new world, to give me a second chance at life, where I can call home and have a safe place to grow and flourish. She gave it all at the price of being alone and lonely for the rest of her life. She passed away with grace and a lonely heart because none of her children were there at her bedside.

A mother's love goes far beyond meeting physical needs. It nourishes the emotional and spiritual core. It means being present in spirit, patient in hardship, and understanding in silence. It's about equipping children with the tools to succeed and nurturing them into compassionate, empathetic, and kind human beings.

I've come to realize it is time to stop blaming my mom and owning up to my mistakes and misunderstanding and start taking responsibility for my own actions, so one day my own children can say the same about me. I've come to realize that my mom's influence on my life has shaped me into who I am today. I'm grateful for that. I'm grateful for the lessons she taught me. I'm deeply grateful for sacrifices she made to shape me to be my authentic self.

Owning up to mistakes and misunderstandings is a sign of growth. It tells the world, "I may have gotten it wrong, but I'm learning and striving to be better." Sometimes it also means saying, "Mom, I misunderstood you. I thought your choices were selfish, when in reality, they were deeply selfless." That kind of honesty is a true marker of strength.

So, what's the solution to the blame game? It's not about eliminating blame entirely—sometimes, someone truly is at fault. But the key lies in approaching problems with a growth mindset: taking ownership of one's actions and being willing to learn from mistakes. It's about accountability, not deflection.

It is hard to understand the actions of others when it does not benefit the individual at that moment, which can lead to feelings of guilt, anxiety, and even shame. And that is exactly how I felt, those feelings can be overwhelming, making it harder to move forward. When I avoided to understand the reason behind her actions, I also missed valuable opportunities for real growth.

Reframing a situation through a more compassionate lens is empowering. It offers a fresh start and a new way forward. By seeking understanding rather than casting blame, doors of opportunities will open—a powerful formula for personal development and lasting transformation. This is liberating.

The blame game is a destructive cycle that impacts individuals across all walks of life. It's a common tendency to shift responsibility for mistakes or misunderstandings onto others instead of taking ownership and embracing personal accountability. However, this habit can have serious consequences damaging relationships, clouding decision-making, and stalling personal growth. Blame fosters resentment, fuels anger and often leads to a breakdown in communication.

Beyond being frustrated, this behavior is deeply harmful. It obstructs self-reflection and stifles learning opportunities. By placing blame externally, individuals implicitly position themselves as flawless—suggesting that fault lies entirely with others.

Here's the thing: the blame game is often a coping mechanism for personal fears and insecurities. By blaming others, people temporarily avoid the discomfort of acknowledging their own failures. People shield themselves from the pain of accountability and the hard work of making amends.

The fear of accountability is rooted deep within the human psyche. Many individuals are afraid of being judged, rejected, or ostracized. There's a discomfort with being perceived as weak or flawed. But what if the script were flipped? What if, instead of assigning blame, one chose to take ownership of mistakes and misunderstandings—recognizing that personal responsibility might play a role?

Taking responsibility isn't just about owning the mistakes; it's about reclaiming control. Acknowledging the capacity to make mistakes—and the willingness to grow from them—fosters resilience. This mindset shift is not only empowering but also essential for genuine personal development.

Taking responsibility for mistakes is not a sign of weakness; it's a profound act of strength. It takes courage to apologize, to make amends, and to confront personal shortcomings. Yet, in doing so, individuals not only repair external relationships but also begin to restore their inner harmony.

So, how can one start taking responsibility for his or her actions and stop playing the blame game?

The first step in navigating any challenging situation is to acknowledge one's role. Taking a step back to reflect on personal actions and identify what could have been done differently lays the groundwork for real change. Responsibility becomes a catalyst for stronger relationships, meaningful personal growth, and improved mental well-being.

Owning mistakes signals accountability and a willingness to learn—qualities that foster deeper trust and mutual respect. It also empowers individuals to take control of their actions and shape their own destiny.

Taking responsibility begins with self-reflection. Step back and evaluate the situation honestly. Acknowledge any emotions involved and recognize missteps without defensiveness. From there, effective communication becomes key. Rather than using accusatory language, speak from personal experience. For instance, instead of saying, "You always do this," try, "I feel frustrated when this happens." This subtle shift in language can lead to much more productive conversations.

Taking responsibility opens the door to growth, learning, and meaningful change. It signals a commitment to personal development and a willingness to do the hard work of becoming better. Owning one's mistakes can be incredibly empowering—like lifting a weight off the shoulders. It creates space to rebuild trust and strengthen relationships.

A crucial part of this process is acknowledging mistakes and offering sincere apologies. This isn't about self-criticism; it's about taking full ownership and using the experience as a learning opportunity. Many people struggle with the art of apology, often leaving behind damaged relationships and unresolved tension. When mistakes go unacknowledged, resentment and mistrust tend to grow. It's easy to fall into a pattern of blame-shifting and defensiveness—hoping the other person will simply understand one's perspective.

But a meaningful apology goes beyond words. It reflects a genuine commitment to growth and accountability. It involves honesty, humility, and action to prevent similar mistakes from happening in the future. Mastering this skill can transform relationships, restore trust, and create a deep sense of personal freedom and empowerment.

The moment of truth arrives when one recognizes that a heartfelt apology can transform relationships and open a path to healing. Taking responsibility for mistakes not only mends connections but also rebuilds trust and credibility. It shows a willingness to listen, learn, and grow. Apologizing is not a sign of weakness—it is a sign of strength and maturity.

For years, the weight of negative thoughts, emotions, anger, and resentment clouded my relationship with my mother. I hadn't realized all that she had done for me. Only recently did my perspective began to shift. I came to understand that taking responsibility for my misunderstandings could lead to forgiveness, self-acceptance, and personal growth.

Through reflection, I began to see things from her point of view. She had always been there sacrificing her own happiness and well-being for my sake. The more I understood her perspective, the more I realized that the apology I owed was not just for my actions. It was also for my attitude and lack of empathy. I needed to say sorry—not just to express regret—but to thank her for all she had done. I needed to acknowledge her sacrifices, to let her know she is seen, valued, and deeply loved.

So today, I want to say thank you, Mom. Thank you for everything you've done for me. Thank you for the sacrifices you've made, for the love you've shown, and for the lessons you've taught. I'm sorry it took me so long to see it, to appreciate it, and to express it.

A Path to Personal Liberation

The journey from blame to personal responsibility is paved with many steps, and one of the most transformative steps is the act of forgiveness. This concept holds such power in personal freedom that it deserves close attention which I dedicated an entire chapter to it. Forgiveness is not a sign of weakness—it's a courageous act of self-liberation. It allows individuals to let go of resentment and anger, breaking free from the emotional prison built by holding on to past wounds. Forgiveness does not excuse harmful behavior; rather, it acknowledges that prolonged bitterness inflicts the most harm on the one who holds it.

True forgiveness often involves self-forgiveness. Everyone makes mistakes. Missteps and moments of pain—whether caused or endured—are part of the human experience. Yet many carry a weight of self-criticism, driven by an inner voice that replays past failures and reinforces guilt. This ongoing cycle of self-blame can stall growth and breed a sense of unworthiness. Self-forgiveness means accepting responsibility without sinking into shame. It involves recognizing imperfections, learning from them, and choosing to move forward with compassion.

This process may include journaling, reflecting on past experiences, and identifying the lessons learned. It's about understanding the context behind certain actions—the pressure, fear, and vulnerability that may have influenced those choices. It's not about erasing the past but integrating it into one's story with awareness and self-compassion.

It's possible to forgive past actions while still acknowledging their consequences and making amends where appropriate. The goal isn't to avoid responsibility, but to release the emotional weight of self-blame that hinders healing and personal growth. For years, the belief that my parents had abandoned me because I was unloved—just another mouth to feed—shaped my decisions. That emotional burden led me to seek love and acceptance in the wrong people and places, resulting in mistakes I could hardly afford.

Forgiveness isn't about denying what happened. It's about weaving the experience into a broader story of learning and transformation. It means letting go of the past's grip and stepping into the present with renewed self-worth.

Forgiving others is a distinct yet equally vital part of the healing process. It demands a significant shift in perspective—a willingness to empathize with those who have caused harm, without excusing their actions. By understanding their motivations, past pain, and personal experiences, individuals can begin to release the anger and resentment that kept them tied to the past. Forgiveness becomes a conscious decision to break the cycle of bitterness and restore inner peace.

Holding onto anger and bitterness only serves to perpetuate the cycle of blame, trapping individuals in a state of emotional turmoil and hindering their ability to move forward. In contrast, forgiveness liberates emotional energy, allowing it to be redirected toward healing and creating a more meaningful future. Ultimately, forgiveness is about letting go of harmful emotions and choosing to prioritize personal well-being.

The process of forgiveness is neither quick nor easy. It unfolds gradually, often marked by emotional setbacks and moments of deep introspection. This journey demands patience, self-compassion, and a willingness to confront difficult emotions. While forgiveness is a deeply personal act, it also contributes to broader collective healing—beginning with an individual's recognition of its transformative power.

Embracing both self-forgiveness and the forgiveness of others paves the way toward greater emotional resilience, inner peace, and a more fulfilling life. Though the path may be challenging, the outcomes are profound: liberation from blame, deeper compassion, and a reclaimed sense of self.

Forgiveness is not a one-size-fits-all experience; rather, it is shaped by intention, the willingness to engage in the process, and the recognition of its profound power to transform lives.

In essence, forgiveness is a journey of self-discovery and healing. It's a powerful tool for dismantling the blame game and reclaiming personal power. It's about breaking free from the prison of resentment and anger, releasing the negative emotions that hold us back, and creating space for growth, understanding, and genuine connection.

This journey of self-discovery is marked by breakthrough moments of self-acceptance and self-empowerment. It is a life-long endeavor—a process of continuous learning, growth, and adaptation. Such a path demands courage, perseverance, and an unwavering commitment to personal development. Yet, the rewards are immeasurable: a richer life, deeper connections, a stronger sense of purpose, and the fulfillment that comes from knowing one is actively shaping their own destiny.

To close, remember this essential truth: we are not defined by our past experiences, but by the choices we make moving forward. Each of us holds the power to shape a future that is meaningful, fulfilling, and aligned with our values. Embrace that power. Step into control. Live with resilience and unshakable self-belief. The journey truly begins when the blame game ends.

Take a moment now to soften the grip of blame and reconnect with your power. This next meditation will guide you toward inner responsibility, emotional freedom, and the peace that comes from releasing what no longer serves you.

CHAPTER THREE

The Self-Acceptance Breakthrough

This chapter is dedicated to everyone who has ever felt the harm and pain of self-doubt, the heavy weight of comparison, or the exhaustion of trying to be someone they're not. To those who have wrestled with the silent battles of inadequacy and the pervasive feeling of *not being enough*, may these pages offer solace, understanding, and a pathway toward embracing the beautiful, unique individual that lies within.

The journey of self-acceptance is not a sprint, but a marathon. May this chapter serve as a compassionate guide and a steadfast companion throughout that process. The hope for the readers to find the strength and courage to unveil their authentic selves and live a life brimming with purpose, joy, and unwavering self-love.

Being authentic in a world that often values conformity can be incredibly difficult. People compare themselves to others, believing that if they can just be more like them, they will be accepted and loved. Many end up wearing masks, pretending to be someone they are not—but deep down, they know it isn't sustainable. That performance becomes exhausting, and eventually, it feels like living a lie.

The whole essence of embracing oneself is deeply connected to self-acceptance. Thoughts like: "There's definitely something wrong with me," "I am not lovable," "I am not enough," or "I do not deserve it," often linger in the mind. These are not just fleeting ideas. They carry heavy emotions such as fear, rejection, resentment, failure, anger, and deep unhappiness. That's where self-acceptance becomes essential.

Self-acceptance is something many strive for, yet it can be incredibly difficult to achieve—especially under the pressures of social media and societal expectations. Still, it's a vital part of personal growth, happiness, and living a harmonious life. Without it, individuals often find themselves stuck in cycles of self-doubt and negativity, making it difficult to move forward.

So, what gets in the way of self-acceptance? For many people, it's the negative self-talk—that inner voice that constantly criticizes, saying they're not good enough or not worthy. Often, individuals become their own worst enemies. Then come societal pressures.

The world around humanity continually dictates what they should be doing, how they should look, and how they should act. There's a constant push to fit into rigid boxes that society has created. On top of that, past trauma, fear of failure, and fear of rejection add more weight. All these factors contribute to the struggles with self-acceptance.

It's important to recognize that being different is what makes each person unique and valuable. Flaws and imperfections are part of what shapes identity—and that's where true beauty lies. When individuals learn to accept themselves as they are, they experience a kind of peace and freedom that's hard to put into words. They begin to live authentically, without apology or pretense. And that, in itself, is incredibly empowering.

Self-acceptance is best understood as a journey—one that doesn't happen overnight. It's a process that requires daily effort, patience, and intention. Taking it one step at a time is not only acceptable, it's essential. There's value in being kind and compassionate toward oneself throughout the process. In the end, that's what truly matters.

Common Barriers to Self-Acceptance

Perfectionism-People are often striving for perfection ... seeking the perfect body, the perfect relationship, the perfect job. When they don't meet these high standards that they've set for themselves, they feel like they're not good enough. Then comes the fear of judgment. Many hide behind a mask of perfectionism, terrified of what others might think. But the truth is, nobody is perfect. Accepting that—recognizing that everyone is figuring it out as they go—can be freeing. And perhaps, much more joyful.

Trying to be perfect, to fit in, or to live up to other people's expectations is exhausting. Individuals get caught up in projecting a certain image or concealing their flaws. In the process, they often lose sight of who they truly are. Constant comparison to others fosters feelings of inadequacy. Society promotes narrow standards of beauty and success, and that pressure can deeply damage self-esteem. It's easy to fall into the belief that one must change in order to belong.

External Validation- Seeking approval is often brushed off as a natural part of life. Human beings are wired to fit in, to be liked, and to feel accepted. However, this desire for approval can become incredibly limiting. It may hold a person back from pursuing passions, taking risks, or showing up as their authentic self.

The impact of seeking approval is far-reaching. It can lead to a constant need for validation, a fear of making the wrong decisions, and a lack of confidence in one's own abilities. People may begin to doubt themselves—questioning whether they are good enough, smart enough, or talented enough. Over time, this can result in a cycle of people-pleasing and decision paralysis driven by the need for external approval.

This need for approval can also lead to indecision. Many become so afraid of making mistakes, of being judged, or of facing rejection that they hesitate to take action. Overthinking, overanalyzing, and second-guessing decisions becomes the norm—often without ever fully committing. As a result, valuable opportunities, meaningful experiences, and personal growth can be lost.

Prioritizing the approval of others often comes at the cost of self-esteem. Instead of defining worth internally, individuals may begin to measure their value based on external opinions. Over time, they may start to believe that their significance depends on others' validation, rather than on their own accomplishments, skills, and talents. This pattern can create a lasting sense of unworthiness, insignificance, and emotional disconnection.

Self-Criticism- Let's take a moment to examine negative self-talk—a challenge that many people face. It's deeply ingrained in the mind, making it difficult to overcome. Often, the focus is on what went wrong or what could have been done better. This constant self-criticism keeps individuals stuck in the past, replaying mistakes and regrets.

But what if the focus shifted? What if, instead, people began recognizing what they did right? Celebrating even the smallest successes could have a profound impact on self-perception and emotional well-being.

Negative self-talk is a major obstacle to self-acceptance. Many individuals become their own harshest critics, punishing themselves over minor mistakes or perceived flaws. They begin to believe they're not good enough or unworthy of love and respect. This cycle is both destructive and difficult to break.

Learning to treat oneself with compassion—and to concentrate on personal strengths rather than shortcomings—is essential. Only through self-acceptance, including acknowledgment of imperfections, can true personal growth begin.

The way one talks to oneself matters. It's remarkable how much inner dialogue can influence self-perception and confidence. When self-talk is rooted in constant criticism, those negative thoughts often begin to shape identity. But when self-compassion is practiced and focus shifts to positive qualities, it's easier to see oneself in a healthier, more empowering light.

It's important to learn to be gentle with oneself and focus on strengths rather than weaknesses. Seeking approval can be a major roadblock. It limits potential, lowers self-esteem, and holds people back from pursuing their passions. The good news? It's entirely possible to break free from the cycle of people-pleasing. Individuals can learn to value their own opinions, trust themselves, and take meaningful action without relying on the validation of others.

When I finally learned to let go of seeking approval, I was able to focus on my own strengths, my own talents, and my own passions. It opened the door to pursue my dreams with confidence—free from fear of rejection or the need for external validation. That is true freedom. And that is the real power of self-acceptance.

Here are three ways to pave the path of true self-acceptance by eliminating barriers: meditation, gratitude, and journaling.

Meditation—a Path to Mind Mastery- Meditation has become a buzzword in recent years — and for good reasons. It's a powerful tool that can transform both life and mind, leading to a more balanced and fulfilling existence. From reducing stress and anxiety to increasing focus and mental clarity, the benefits of meditation are far-reaching.

Everyone has been there stuck in traffic, feeling anxious about a big presentation, or stressed over a looming deadline. Life can feel overwhelming, and it's easy to get swept up in the chaos. But there is a way to calm the storm and discover inner peace.

Meditation offers a powerful coping mechanism for navigating life's challenges with greater ease and confidence. Without it, individuals are often left struggling with negative emotions and thoughts that can hold them back from reaching their full potential.

In today's fast-paced world, it's easy to get caught up in the hustle and bustle and forget to prioritize personal well-being.

With constant connection to devices, social media, and the news, many individuals are left feeling drained and exhausted.

Meditation offers a much-needed break from the chaos. It provides an opportunity to step back, breathe, and recharge. This practice is a powerful way to regain control over mental and emotional health, promoting a more balanced and fulfilling life.

One of the greatest benefits of meditation is its ability to enhance focus and mental clarity. In a world filled with constant stimuli, staying attentive can be challenging. Meditation trains the mind to remain present and focused—even amid distraction. It's an effective tool for improving productivity, creativity, and overall mental performance.

There are many different types of meditation techniques, each offering its own unique benefits. One of the most popular is **mindfulness meditation**, which involves paying attention to the present moment without judgment. **Guided meditation** is another widely used technique, where individuals follow the guidance of a teacher or a recording to achieve a specific mental state. **Transcendental meditation** takes a more spiritual approach, using a mantra to quiet the mind and access deeper levels of consciousness.

The key to starting a meditation practice is to begin small and stay consistent. Short sessions—just five to ten minutes a day—can be effective, and the duration can gradually increase as comfort with the practice grows. It's also helpful to find a quiet, comfortable space free from distractions. Some may prefer using a guided recording, while others might simply focus on their breath. Either approach is valid, depending on what feels most natural.

I want to share a friend's powerful personal story that really drives home the transformative power of meditation. A close friend of mine was struggling with anxiety and depression, feeling lost and disconnected from the world around her. She started meditating daily, and within a few weeks, she noticed a significant shift in her mood and outlook. She felt more grounded, more present, and more connected to herself and others. Meditation gave her the tools she needed to take control of her mental health and live a more fulfilling life.

But meditation isn't just about reducing stress and anxiety—it's also a powerful tool for personal growth and transformation. By quieting the mind and accessing a deeper state of consciousness, individuals can tap into inner wisdom and gain a deeper understanding of themselves and the world around them. Meditation also helps in recognizing patterns and habits that may be holding one back, opening the door to positive change and a more authentic way of living.

Gratitude—The Secret to Happiness and Success. When gratitude is cultivated, it opens the door to a life filled with happiness, success, and fulfillment. This mindset shifts focus from what's missing to what's already present—and it's an incredibly powerful tool for achieving goals.

One of the biggest challenges many people face when it comes to gratitude is recognizing and practicing it daily. It's easy to get caught up in busy schedules, stress, anxiety, and endless to-do lists—making it difficult to step back and appreciate what's good. The tendency is often to focus on what's going wrong, what's missing, or what's wished for, rather than acknowledging what is already present.

Another common challenge is taking things for granted. When certain comforts or relationships become routine, it's easy to stop noticing their value. The beauty around us, the people who care, and the opportunities available can fade into the background. Entitlement can quietly replace appreciation—and that's when the sense of what truly matters begins to blur.

Another common obstacle to practicing gratitude is that it can feel forced or inauthentic. People may try to cultivate a sense of thankfulness, but it doesn't always feel genuine. Thoughts like, *"I'm supposed to be grateful for my health, but I'm really frustrated with this cold right now,"* or *"I should appreciate my job, but I can't stand my boss,"* are not uncommon. It can be difficult to reconcile negative emotions with the concept of gratitude.

However, gratitude isn't about ignoring challenges or pretending everything is fine. It's about recognizing that even during difficult moments, there is still something to appreciate. It involves shifting focus from what is missing to what is already present—and finding beauty in that perspective.

Gratitude has a meaningful impact on mental well-being. Regular practice can help rewire the brain to notice the positive, which may lead to increased happiness, lower stress and anxiety levels, and better sleep. It can also strengthen relationships, as appreciating others deepens emotional bonds and fosters stronger connections.

Gratitude can also have a huge impact on overall life satisfaction. When individuals focus on what they already have—rather than what they lack—they begin to feel more content, more at peace, and more fulfilled. They start to appreciate the little things and find joy in everyday moments. And when people are grateful for what they have, they're more likely to take care of it and make the most of it.

I'll never forget the time I was going through a tough breakup. I was feeling lost, alone, and completely heartbroken. But one day, I sat down and wrote a list of all the things I was grateful for—my health, my friends, my family, my home. Even in the midst of pain and heartache, gratitude revealed how much remained to be thankful for. That realization was transformative.

From that day on, a conscious effort to practice gratitude daily began. I started a gratitude journal, where I wrote down three things I was grateful for each day. And it changed my life. I started to see my life in a different way—the world slowly came into focus as a place of abundance rather than scarcity. Small moments became sources of joy. And gradually, I started to feel more at peace, more content, and more fulfilled.

Journaling—A Life-Changing Practice. Journaling has become increasingly popular, and for good reasons. Many are beginning to recognize the incredible impact it can have on mental and emotional well-being.

In today's world, stress and anxiety are at an all-time high. The constant noise of social media, the pressure to perform, and the never-ending to-do lists often leave people feeling overwhelmed and unclear about their priorities. It's easy to get stuck in a cycle of negativity, self-doubt, and uncertainty. While many seek ways to calm their minds, they often don't know where to start. That stuck feeling is becoming more common—and it's affecting nearly every area of life.

The mind can feel like a cluttered room—thoughts, emotions, and experiences jumbled together. It becomes difficult to make sense of anything during that chaos. People may struggle to identify their strengths, passions, and goals. They feel lost, and it's an unsettling place to be. But there is a way to quiet the noise, untangle the mess, and find some much-needed clarity.

What if journaling could be the game-changer someone's been searching for? It's a powerful tool that helps process emotions, gain perspective, and unlock untapped potential. This section explores five powerful reasons why journaling can make a lasting impact.

Reason number one: Journaling clarifies thoughts and feelings. Putting pen to paper begins to unravel the tangled web of emotions and ideas swirling around in the mind. Patterns and habits start to emerge, and areas for improvement become clearer. It can be incredibly liberating to finally understand what's been holding a person back.

Reason number two: Journaling reduces stress and anxiety. Studies show that writing down worries can calm the nervous system and reduce feelings of overwhelm. It's like a weight has been lifted—offering a sense of lightness, freedom, and renewed control.

Reason number three: Journaling helps set and achieve goals. When objectives are written down, they become tangible, forming a roadmap for success. Many are surprised at how focused and motivated they become when there's a clear direction.

Reason number four: Journaling increases self-awareness. It supports the development of a deeper understanding of one's values, strengths, and weaknesses. Patterns, triggers, and motivations become easier to recognize. It's a powerful experience to understand oneself on a deeper level.

Reason number five: Journaling fosters creativity and inspiration. When individuals allow themselves to express freely, they tap into a deep well of creativity and imagination. The ideas, insights, and inspiration that begin to flow onto the page can be truly surprising.

A powerful story of a client of mine illustrates the transformative impact of journaling. It comes from someone who was struggling with anxiety and depression but found solace in the simple act of writing. He began journaling every day, pouring his heart and soul onto the page. Slowly but surely, he started to heal. Over time, he began to see the world through a new lens—feeling more confident, more hopeful, and more at peace.

It's incredible to consider that something as accessible as journaling can make such a profound difference. The five reasons presented here are just the beginning, the possibilities are truly endless. So, here's a challenge: try journaling and see how it can transform life. It may lead to unexpected and beautiful places.

One of the most transformative truths is that self-acceptance isn't a destination, it's a journey. It's a daily practice, something to return to in every moment. It means being kind to oneself, focusing on strengths rather than weaknesses. It's about celebrating individuality and embracing the true self, flaws and all. In doing so, the door to a life of freedom, happiness, and deeper connection with others will be opened.

To recap, embracing one's true self is about accepting who they are—without apology or pretense. It's about cultivating self-compassion, challenging negative beliefs, and celebrating individuality. It's not always easy, but it's absolutely worth it.

Maintaining self-acceptance is a lifelong journey. It's a continuous process of learning, growth, and adaptation. Embrace the ups and downs, the challenges and triumphs.

Remember that self-acceptance is not a passive state; it's an active practice, requiring consistent effort and self-compassion.

By cultivating self-awareness, embracing change, challenging negative self-talk, building a supportive network, and celebrating the progress, one can nurture a profound and lasting sense of self-acceptance that will enrich every aspect of life. Remember, you are worthy of love, acceptance, and happiness, precisely as you are, right now, imperfections and all. Embrace this truth and watch your life transform.

You've explored the truth of who you are — now it's time to embrace it fully. Let the following meditation hold you in self-love, helping you release comparison and rest in the worthiness you already carry.

Part Two: Evolve-Let it Be

With foundation of radical self-acceptance now established, the next journey invites individual to evolve—gently, intentionally, lovingly, and gracefully. As self-love deepens in alignment with authentic self, a strong sense of worth begins to take root. Individuals begin to understand that they are worthy—of love, of peace, of joy, and of a life that reflects their truth.

From this place of clarity, healthy boundaries begin to form. Energy is protected, time is honored, and emotional well-being is prioritized. Relationships are chosen with intention—those that uplift and align, rather than deplete or distract.

As this truth settles into the heart, the invitation is to pause, breathe, and listen. The guided mediation that follows is designed to anchor this shift, allowing the frequency to awaken healing from within. This is where inner growth becomes inner peace. Evolve, immerse, and let it be.

CHAPTER FOUR

The Power of Discovering Authenticity

This chapter is dedicated to the countless individuals who have bravely embarked on journeys of self-discovery, often in the face of immense challenges and societal pressures. It honors those who have questioned conventional definitions of success and happiness, choosing instead a path rooted in purpose and inner peace.

To those who have chosen vulnerability over conformity, self-compassion over self-criticism, and selfless contribution over self-serving ambition, a true testament of courage and resilience.

The question that many struggle to answer for most of their life is, "How do I discover my authentic self? How do I know what that even looks like?" The short answer lies in this powerful truth: *"Whatever I do must make me happy ..."*

as opposed to, *"There is a price for my happiness that I have to pay with my soul."*

When someone begins living authentically, they no longer act with expectations from others. Instead, they do what they do for the greater good—of their family, community, and the world—without expecting anything in return. And that choice, more than anything, brings a deep and lasting sense of joy.

But it's rarely easy at first. Many believe that the more they give, the more they'll be appreciated. They offer love freely, without expecting it in return, only to feel depleted. When they finally ask for love or attention, they're often labeled as "needy" or accused of complaining too much.

In that cycle, they keep pouring from an empty cup—until it starts to show. The emotional exhaustion sets in, physical energy fades, and mental health begins to suffer. And all too often, they're told the pain is their fault.

But discovering one's authentic self is often the turning point. It becomes the key to unlocking personal fulfillment and happiness. It lays the foundation for a life that truly resonates— one that is authentic, meaningful, and filled with purpose.

It's a moment to stop trying to fit into someone else's idea of happiness and start finding one's own intention and purpose. A moment to stop chasing someone else's definition of beauty and begin defining it from within. A moment to stop molding oneself to someone else's idea of success—and start creating a life that feels genuinely true.

Many people struggle to find their true selves. Child-hood traumas are often buried deep inside. Layers of grief, guilt, anger, and resentment weigh heavily. Intuition is rarely trusted, and few take the time to look deep within to uncover the root causes of the negative energy that lingers in daily life.

Added to that is the constant bombardment of societal pressure—messages about who one should be and how one should act. The opinions of others often dictate personal choices, leading to compromises in values just to fit in.

There is a common fear of standing out, of being different, of embracing individuality. But it is this very fear that prevents people from living authentically. Conforming to expectations can suppress creativity, passion, and personal identity. The masks worn to impress others eventually disconnect individuals from who they truly are.

Breaking free from these constraints and beginning to live an authentic life starts with these two vital steps: self-reflection and self-compassion.

Self-reflection is taking time to understand what drives a person, what they stand for, and what they truly want from life. This is essential. This is where mindfulness becomes a powerful tool—it helps cultivate awareness, reduce stress, and unlock untapped potential.

By being present in the moment, individuals can tune into their thoughts and emotions, gaining deeper self-understanding. The noise of the outside world begins to fade, allowing space for the inner voice to be heard. Feelings can be acknowledged, patterns recognized, and decisions made with intention—aligned with personal values and goals.

Embracing vulnerability is equally important. It involves taking risks, facing the possibility of criticism or rejection, and being open enough to share one's fears, dreams, and personal story. It's about having the courage to be imperfect, to make mistakes, and to grow from them.

Self-reflection is an ongoing journey—not a final destination. It demands courage, self-acceptance, and the willingness to evolve. It calls for embracing imperfections and celebrating individuality. Though the path may be challenging, the reward is a life lived with authenticity and purpose—a life that reflects the truth of who a person truly is.

Self-compassion is essential for self-discovery. It allows individuals to approach themselves with kindness, understanding, and patience. By being gentle to oneself, it becomes possible to let go of self-criticism, embrace imperfections, and develop a more loving relationship with the self. Discovering one's true nature is a vital step toward living a purposeful and fulfilling life.

One of the most powerful self-compassion exercises is practicing loving-kindness meditation. This involves repeating phrases such as "May I be happy, may I be healthy, may I be at peace," either silently or aloud, directed toward oneself or others. It may seem simple, but it is remarkably effective in cultivating kindness and compassion inwardly.

Another valuable exercise is writing a letter from the perspective of a compassionate friend. What would a caring friend say to someone struggling or experiencing difficult emotions? Those same words are exactly what should be offered inwardly in times of personal challenge.

There was a time in my life that was marked by anxiety and deep self-doubt. Feelings of overwhelm and failure constantly circled in my mind. But then I realized that I was being incredibly harsh and critical towards myself—expecting perfection and offering no grace when those expectations weren't met. I realized the importance of practicing self-compassion, to treat myself with kindness and understanding, rather than criticism and judgment. It was a turning point for me.

With consistent practice of self-compassion, a noticeable shift occurred. Confidence grew, resilience strengthened, and a sense of inner peace began to emerge. It became evident that worthiness wasn't tied to accomplishments or achievements, but to the simple fact of being human. And that's the truth—everyone is human, everyone makes mistakes, and everyone struggles at times.

Here are four powerful steps to finding authentic self:

1. Reflect on Values and Beliefs
2. Finding Passion and Interests
3. Evolve from Vulnerability to Authenticity
4. Create a Roadmap for Personal Growth

Number One—Reflect on Values and Beliefs: It's essential to take time to reflect on personal values and beliefs. In the hustle and bustle of daily life, it's easy to get swept up and lose sight of what truly matters. Yet, taking even a moment for honest reflection can have a powerful impact on personal growth and development.

One of the biggest challenges many people face is aligning daily actions with their core values. There are things often stated as important. However, when life picks up speed, societal pressures and distractions take over. It's common to get caught up in the busy-ness of life, only to realize later that one's actions no longer reflect their true beliefs. This disconnect can lead to feelings of guilt, shame, or even anxiety, as individuals struggle to reconcile how they live with what they believe.

Many experience this disconnect firsthand. For example, someone might claim to value relationships yet find themselves constantly checking their phone instead of being fully present with loved ones. Or they might prioritize health in words but consistently choose convenience over nourishing the body. Recognizing this misalignment is difficult—but it's also the first meaningful step toward change.

The truth is, everyone is a work in progress, and it's okay to acknowledge when personal standards aren't being met. What truly matters is taking the time to reflect on one's values and making intentional decisions about how to show up in the world.

When it comes to reflecting on values, there are many different methods people can use. Some find journaling to be a powerful tool, as it allows thoughts and feelings to be processed on paper. Others prefer meditation or quiet contemplation, which helps them tap into their inner wisdom. Some even engage in conversations with friends or peers, gaining new perspectives and insights through shared dialogue.

One helpful approach is to schedule regular reflection time into daily routine. This might be as simple as taking 10 minutes each morning to focus on gratitude and daily intentions, or setting aside an hour on the weekend to look back on the previous week and identify areas for growth in the days ahead.

Reflecting on values can have a profound impact on decision-making. When individuals are clear about what matters most to them, they are more likely to make choices that align with those values. They're more likely to say no to things that don't serve them, and yes to things that do. This clarity often leads to a stronger sense of purpose and direction, as life begins to reflect what truly matters.

One memorable example involved a client of mine who shared her story. She was stuck in a job that didn't align with her values. Although the pay was good, she was miserable—and it was taking a toll on her mental and physical health. With a great deal of courage, she eventually took a leap of faith and pursued a career that reflected her deeper beliefs. It wasn't easy, but it turned out to be one of the best decisions she ever made.

That experience highlights how essential it is to live in alignment with personal values. When actions and beliefs are in harmony, people are more likely to feel fulfilled, happy, and at peace. They wake up each morning with enthusiasm for the day ahead—rather than dread.

Number Two—Finding Passion and Interests: Finding passion and a true calling in life is a concept often discussed but rarely achieved. But what does it really mean to discover one's passion, and how does it connect to uncovering a deeper purpose in life? For many, it feels like the holy grail of self-discovery — the key to unlocking a life filled with fulfillment and happiness.

Identifying passion can be a challenge, and it's easy to see why. With so many options available, it can feel overwhelming to even know where to begin. Society constantly bombards individuals with messages about what they should be doing — from social media to well-meaning friends and family. Added to that is the fear of choosing the wrong path — the fear of failure that can leave a person stuck in place.

Many people express feeling as if they're drifting through life without purpose or direction. They find themselves doing what they think they *should* do, rather than what they truly want. It's a common struggle — and a painful one — because there's so much more to life than simply going through the motions.

Everyone holds the potential to live a life that aligns with who they truly are. But doing so requires courage, clarity, and the willingness to challenge the status quo.

But what if it were possible to break free from this cycle of uncertainty and discover true passions and interests? For some, it's a process of self-reflection—taking time to quiet the mind and listen to that inner voice. For others, it involves trying new activities and stepping outside their comfort zones. And then there are those who seek feedback from others—asking for input and guidance from trusted voices. The key is to find what works individually and to stay open to the process of discovery.

One of the most powerful ways to uncover passion is by trying new things. It can be scary—putting oneself out there and risking failure. But it's often in those uncertain moments that people discover what they're truly capable of. Even if the perfect fit isn't found right away, the journey itself reveals valuable insights.

There was a time in my life when I felt completely lost—unsure of which direction to go. Being stuck in a draining job made every day feel like going through the motions. But then, I look a risk to pursue a long-standing interest: writing.

It was daunting—not knowing whether the talent was there, or if it could ever become a livelihood. But something about the experience felt right. It sparked a fire in me that had long been missing. That one decision transformed everything, offering a renewed sense of purpose and direction.

That moment of discovery felt like a weight had been lifted. It was as if life had finally aligned with a deeper truth, bringing an overwhelming sense of freedom and authenticity. It was liberating. It's a feeling many long for—a sense of purpose and fulfillment that brings clarity and peace.

Finding one's passion and true calling begins with being open to the process of discovery. It involves trying new things, welcoming feedback, and listening closely to that inner voice. The journey isn't always easy, but it's undoubtedly worth it. When someone begins living in alignment with their true self, everything starts to fall into place, and life feels more meaningful—just as it's meant to be.

Number Three—Evolve from Vulnerability into Authenticity: When people think about living a happy and fulfilling life, the focus often falls on external factors like success, wealth, or status. But the key to unlocking true happiness and meaningful connections often lies in something much more internal—the ability to be vulnerable and authentic. These two concepts are closely intertwined and embracing them can open a world of possibilities.

Many individuals experience a deep fear of vulnerability. There's often a fear of being rejected, judged, or hurt for showing one's true self to the world. Letting down one's guard can feel risky, opening the door to potential hurt or the perception of weakness.

This fear is understandable, but it can also be incredibly limiting. Without vulnerability, the chance to form deep and meaningful relationships is lost. Connections remain superficial, leaving people feeling unseen or misunderstood.

Most have, at some point, found themselves pretending to be someone else just to fit in or be accepted. This constant effort to maintain a facade is exhausting and can take a toll on mental and emotional well-being. But breaking free from that cycle—choosing instead to embrace imperfection and show up authentically—can be transformative. Vulnerability carries the risk of hurt, but it also creates space for love, acceptance, and true connection.

The fear of vulnerability is often rooted in the fear of rejection. People are afraid that if they put themselves out there, they'll be judged harshly or pushed away. But rejection is a natural part of life—it happens whether someone is being open or guarded. So why not take the chance to be authentic and true to oneself, even if it means facing rejection along the way?

Vulnerability often leads to personal growth and deeper self-awareness. It requires individuals to confront their own flaws and imperfections, offering the opportunity to grow and become better versions of themselves. It also fosters empathy and compassion for others, as those who have been vulnerable understand what it feels like to be hurt or exposed.

I'll never forget the time when I finally worked up the courage to share my struggles with anxiety with a close friend. It was terrifying, because I was afraid of being judged or rejected. But instead, my friend was incredibly supportive and understanding.

She shared her own struggles with me, and we formed a bond that was deeper and more meaningful than anything I had experienced before. It was a powerful reminder that vulnerability is the key and opens the door to true connection and emotional fulfillment.

In that moment, there was a sense of relief—as if a weight had lifted. Being able to fully be myself without fear of judgment was incredibly freeing. That experience revealed a lasting truth: vulnerability is a strength, not a weakness. It takes courage to open up and it's a skill that can be cultivated over time.

Number Four—Create a Roadmap for Personal Growth: (Please visit my website **www.KobiJulian.com** for a free 28 transformational eBook, or a Goal Getter Planner) Having a personal growth plan is crucial for achieving success and fulfillment. It serves as a roadmap that helps individuals identify areas for improvement, set realistic goals, and stay focused on what truly matters. With a well-crafted plan, it's easier to overcome obstacles, build new habits, and make steady progress toward meaningful goals—ultimately leading to the discovery of one's authentic self.

Many people start the year with high hopes and ambitions, only to fall back into old patterns and habits. Why does this happen? Often, it's due to a lack of clear goals, no system for tracking progress, or simply a loss of motivation over time.

Fear can also be a major obstacle—fear of failure, fear of change, or fear of the unknown. Procrastination is another common barrier, often leading to guilt and shame, which make it even harder to get back on track. Self-doubt can also creep in, quietly undermining even the best intentions and efforts.

When these obstacles are combined, it's no surprise that many individuals struggle to make lasting changes in their lives. The good news is that with a solid personal growth plan, these challenges can be overcome, and real progress toward meaningful goals becomes possible.

Creating a personalized growth plan begins with identifying what one hopes to achieve. What are the goals and values? What kind of person one is hoping to become? What kind of life one wants to lead? It's important to take time to reflect on these questions and write down the answers.

The next step involves breaking down those goals into smaller, actionable steps. What specific habits need to be built—or broken? What skills are essential to develop? What kind of support system should be in place? Once the plan is clearly defined, it's time to take action. There's no need to worry too much about mistakes—moving forward and being present is the true focus here.

One of the most impactful strategies for personal growth is a shift in mindset. Rather than focusing on what isn't working, it helps to recognize what is. Instead of dwelling on weaknesses, attention should be directed toward strengths. And rather than comparing oneself to others, the focus should remain on personal progress.

Another key strategy is to build accountability. It's advisable for individuals to share their goals with a trusted friend or mentor and ask them to help by holding them accountable. Alternatively, joining a community of like-minded individuals can offer support and motivation.

When beginning a personal growth plan, it's important to remember that starting small is perfectly okay. Rather than trying to tackle everything at once, it's more effective to focus on one or two areas initially and then build from there. It's also important not to be too hard on oneself after a setback—just get back on track and keep moving forward.

Let this next meditation become your sacred space to return to yourself — the truest version, the one beneath the noise. As you listen, may you reconnect with the real you, the one who's been waiting to be seen and celebrated.

CHAPTER FIVE

The Power of Forgiveness

This chapter is dedicated to those who have bravely faced their pain, to those on the verge of taking that first step toward forgiveness, and to those who have already experienced the life-altering effects of letting go. May the following pages serve as a beacon of hope, a guide on the journey, and a source of strength and encouragement as readers navigate the complexities of emotional healing.

It is the sincere hope of this work that these pages empower individuals to embrace the transformative power of forgiveness and embark on a path toward a more fulfilling and joyful life. For in the act of forgiving, one ultimately forgives oneself and unlocks the boundless potential for happiness that lies within.

Forgiveness has the power to change lives in ways that may seem unimaginable. It's not always easy, and it's rarely comfortable—but the rewards are well worth the effort. Choosing to forgive means taking back control, breaking free from the weight of the past, and opening the heart to new experiences and relationships.

It's a process that can be incredibly difficult, but the healing that comes from it is priceless. When someone is hurt or betrayed, it's natural to feel resentment and anger toward the one responsible. There may even be a sense of entitlement to hold onto those emotions, as if forgiving would signal weakness. But the truth is, holding onto resentment only causes harm in the long run. It drains energy, damages relationships, and prevents moving forward in life.

A while back I forgave my mother thinking what she had done to me was unjust and cruel. It wasn't until recently that I realized I needed to ask for forgiveness from her, for thinking that she was wrong and all my suffering is because of what she had done. The truth is that I am the one who needed forgiveness, for not understanding the depth of her sacrifice.

Years ago, I was betrayed by someone I truly and deeply trusted. It felt as though the world had turned upside down, leaving no clear path forward. But as forgiveness began to take root, the emotional burden started to lift. I felt more at peace, more grounded, and more able to move forward with my life.

These powerful personal stories illustrate the life-changing effects of forgiveness. These experiences taught me that forgiveness isn't just about the other person – it's about me, and my own healing. It's about taking back control of my life, and choosing to let go of the pain and resentment that's holding me back. Forgiveness gave me a sense of freedom and empowerment that I'd never experienced before, and it's something I'll always be grateful for.

Forgiveness can be challenging because it requires individuals to confront their own emotions and vulnerabilities. While it's uncomfortable to face personal pain and weakness, doing so is a necessary step in the healing process. Choosing to forgive means choosing to understand those emotions and to reclaim control of one's life.

One of the biggest challenges people face when it comes to forgiving others is the feeling of justified anger. It often feels like there's every right to be angry, and that offering forgiveness would mean letting the other person off the hook. In truth, forgiveness isn't about the other person at all. It's about personal healing. Forgiveness is not granted for someone else's sake—it's for the benefit of the one who forgives.

Another common challenge is the fear of being hurt again. After experiencing pain, it's natural to build emotional walls as a form of protection. However, those same walls can prevent deeper connections with others. Forgiveness helps dismantle those barriers and opens the door to new experiences and relationships.

On the other hand, forgiveness has many benefits, it opens the door to a range of psychological growth. It reduces stress and anxiety, improves mental well-being, and even strengthens the immune system. It also has the power to transform relationships, helping individuals form deeper connections and build stronger, more meaningful bonds.

One of the most profound benefits of forgiveness is the sense of freedom it creates. Holding onto resentment keeps a person tied to the past, constantly reliving pain and hurt. But choosing to forgive lifts that burden. Emotions no longer weigh down the heart, allowing space to heal and move forward in life.

Physical and mental scars can begin to heal through the power of forgiveness. Consider the story of a remarkable woman who found healing in her body by first forgiving herself. Her name is Maria, and she shared her experience in her own words:

"I grew up in the 60s. I had a high school experience like a lot of girls dream about. I got pregnant my junior year in high school, got kicked out of high school. I had to finish high school with pregnant girls and delinquent boys. That was a very, very rough period for me. And I was unknowingly accumulating a great deal of self-loathing and stress during that time."

"Few months later, after the birth of my daughter, I learned that I had severe and rare kidney disease, and only had a few months to live, I ended in an intensive care unit. I am only 18 years of age by now, with a child and not married, and certainly not financially in the right place. My seven-month-old daughter and her father are staying at my parents' home."

"A woman came to my room the night before the procedure where the doctors had to remove my right kidney and talked to me. To this day, I do not know who she was, but I call her my Guardian Angel. She said would you tell me what's going on in your life and share your story with me?"

"I shared my story with her. I told her that I was expelled from school because I was pregnant." She said, "Maria, I've heard how much you've been despising yourself, even though you've told me how much you adore your little kid. You feel as though you have embarrassed your family, your school, and yourself. For more than a year, you have been harboring strong emotions of self-loathing and self-rejection, and those ideas are poisonous to your body. And your body is displaying all of these toxins through an illness."

She asked, "Is it possible that the vibration you're experiencing and the outcome you're getting are related?" Maria thought to herself, "Well, no one I know believed this to be." She continued with her story, "she then provided me with a tool that allowed me to think in a different way and replace my harmful way of thinking." She asked, "Would you be willing to do an experiment that if you do it, it's actually your best shot at living the life you would love living."

"When she asked me what I would do if I could live if I didn't die, I knew immediately what I would do. I would raise my little girl, and I wanted to be a teacher. I'd wanted to be a teacher from the time I was a little girl." Then she said, "Okay. Hold on to that vision. Together, let's envision that. After you have the surgery, you're going to have some pain. As the pain eases, your mind is going to want to go down those well-worn paths of thinking. They're like ruts in the road, and thoughts just want to keep doing the same kind of flow."

She continued, "So you're going to have to interrupt the thoughts that are constrictive. So, here's what I want you to do. When you notice yourself beginning to think a self-loathing thought, say, 'No.' We're going to sweep all that up. We're going to put it in the kidney, and when this kidney's removed, instead of getting worse, let's imagine you're going to get better. It's worth an experiment, she says."

"So, imagine that you're holding your little girl's hand. She said, "Think a self-loathing thought, say, 'No, that left with the kidney.' Then you have your little girl's hand in yours and you're walking up to a school. She's five years old. Feel that warmth of her hand in your hand. There's a kindergarten teacher welcoming her. She goes into class, and you go down the hallway, click, click, click. Around the corner is your classroom. And you are a teacher."

She continued this visual imagination, "And you fast forward in your mind and you're in a big stadium or an auditorium, and you look around and you see all these caps and gowns. You hear your daughter's name called, and she walks across the stage, gets her diploma, holds it up, and you're cheering. And you're so proud of all the moments you've had to help her get here."

"And then you fast forward in your mind, and you're sitting in the front row of a wedding, and it's your daughter's. She's marrying the love of her life. You're the mother of the bride. You're sitting in the front row of the wedding, and your teaching career is flourishing." She said, "Just keep repeating that."

"So, the surgery came, I went through it with all these visualizations. Yup, a couple weeks later my numbers were stable enough that the doctor said, 'Well…maybe you're going to have a little more than six months. Maybe if we go to the urologist three or four times a week, you could go home for a little while until you have to come back in.'"

Maria continued with her story, "I went home in an ambulance I was so sick. I couldn't even lift my head off the pillow. But over time, my numbers not only stabilized, they also just started slightly improving and improving and improving."

"Four or five months later, I'm sitting with the doctor, the surgeon, the specialist, the general practitioner, and they're all looking at my numbers. And they're shaking their heads saying, 'We don't have any science to explain what has happened with you. But whatever you're doing, keep doing it. We're going to write medical anomaly on your chart.' Well, I actually didn't really know yet what I was doing. But it was a form of forgiveness."

If the mind and thought can make a person sick, then the mind and thought can also bring healing. Sometimes, forgiveness feels like a leap of faith. It may not feel like the right time to forgive, or the emotions might still be difficult to process. But the truth is, forgiveness is a journey—and it's perfectly okay to take it one step at a time. Forgiveness doesn't have to happen overnight, but it does begin with a willingness to take that first step.

There are times in life that one needs to learn to give and receive forgiveness in a toxic relationship. These toxic relationships can be incredibly draining, and it's easy to understand why. They act like a slow poison, seeping into the mind and heart—leaving a person feeling worthless, unloved, and unappreciated. Despite the pain they cause, it's common to feel stuck, unable to break free.

The emotional and psychological toll of toxic relationships is staggering. Anxiety, depression, and low self-esteem are just a few of the effects. But perhaps the most damaging impact is the overwhelming sense of being trapped in a cycle of pain and suffering with no clear way out.

One of the greatest challenges in letting go of a toxic relationship is the guilt or sense of responsibility that often accompanies it. There may be a belief that staying is necessary to fix the other person or to make them happy. But the truth is, no one can fix another person, and happiness cannot be created for someone else. The real responsibility lies in self-care—prioritizing personal well-being and emotional health.

So why do people stay in these relationships? Why choose to suffer in silence rather than take a stand and break free? Often the answer is simple—fear. Fear of being alone, of not being loved, of not being enough. But the truth is—every person is enough, just as they are. Everyone deserves to be loved, respected, and happy.

Forgiveness isn't about forgetting what happened or excusing someone's behavior. It's about releasing their hold and reclaiming personal power. Forgiveness is not for the other person—it's for the one letting go. It's a conscious decision to release pain and anger, and to step into a brighter, more positive future.

Forgiveness is a powerful tool that brings freedom and liberation. It's not always easy. It takes time, effort, and the courage to confront pain and emotions. But the reward is real: a life free from the chains of toxic relationships, filled with love, peace, and happiness.

I'll never forget the story of a client who spent years in a toxic relationship. She was constantly belittled and put down by her partner, always feeling like she had to walk on eggshells. One day, though, she found the courage to leave and began building a new life.

It wasn't easy. She wrestled with guilt and shame and had to relearn how to love herself. But over time, she began to heal and rediscover happiness. When she did, it was as if a weight had been lifted from her shoulders—she was finally free, she could breathe again.

Forgiveness is not a one-time event; it's a process—one that requires time, patience, and practice. But the outcome is worth it: a life no longer defined by pain, now filled with love, peace, and hope. For those trying to break free from a toxic relationship, forgiveness may very well be the key to true freedom.

Here are a few steps to start the forgiveness process. The first step in forgiveness is recognizing the impact of anger. Holding onto anger is like carrying a toxin that poisons the mind and body from within. It affects relationships, mental health, and even physical well-being. Once the effects of anger are understood, the importance of forgiveness becomes clearer.

Another helpful approach is reframing thoughts. Anger can distort thinking, making others seem malicious or intentionally harmful. But shifting perspective allows for the possibility that the other person may have been acting from their own pain or struggles.

Empathy is also a powerful tool in the forgiveness process. Trying to understand another person's experience can be deeply freeing. It's not about justifying a harmful behavior. It's about acknowledging shared humanity.

I'll always remember the moment I truly forgave someone who had caused me deep pain. It was as if a heavy burden had been lifted—I felt lighter, freer, and able to breathe again. Forgiveness is a journey, and it does not come easily. But by acknowledging the toll that anger was taking on me, shifting my perspective, and choosing to lead with empathy, I found liberation from the grip of resentment.

For a long time, I wrestled with the weight if self-forgiveness. I carried the burden of past mistakes, holding myself hostage to shame and guilt. I found it hard to extend grace inward, to speak to myself with kindness, or to fully embrace and evolve into the women I was created to be.

But then something sacred shifted within me. I came to understand that perfection was never the goal—wholeness was. And in that moment, I discovered a deeper truth: my worth was never tied to what I've done or failed to do. My value was never rooted in performance—it was anchored in my identity. I am valuable simply because I AM. And that was a game-changer.

The lesson to be learned from forgiveness is rarely easy, but it's often powerful. When self-forgiveness begins—when the weight of shame and regret starts to lift—freedom follows. Life begins to feel beautiful again. There's space to simply exist, without apology or excuse. And that's an incredibly liberating experience.

The breakthrough came when I finally understood that I was worthy of forgiveness—not because I had earned it, but simply because I am human. That truth landed in my spirit and changed everything. In that sacred moment, I no longer needed to strive for perfection or punish myself for my past. I saw myself with compassion and grace. I realized I could forgive myself, fully and freely, just as I am. And that realization became the beginning of true healing.

Self-forgiveness is a concept that is often overlooked, yet it plays a vital role in personal growth and mental well-being. Holding onto guilt, shame, and negative self-talk can be paralyzing, making it difficult to move forward and live the life one truly desires.

One of the most common struggles with self-forgiveness is the overwhelming sense of guilt. Many replay those "what-if" moments, blaming themselves for not making different choices. This toxic cycle can lead to feelings of inadequacy and low self-worth.

Shame is another heavy burden. It often shows up as self-doubt, anxiety, and even depression. People tend to be their own harshest critics—magnifying flaws and mistakes so much so that letting go of the past feels impossible. Negative self-talk adds to the weight, with inner dialogue that chips away at confidence and makes self-forgiveness seem out of reach.

Moreover, the fear of being vulnerable and open with oneself can make it difficult to confront mistakes and take responsibility. It often feels easier to blame external circumstances or others, rather than acknowledging a personal role in the situation.

For me, the struggle with self-forgiveness was very real. Growing up, I always put immense pressure on myself to be perfect, to never make mistakes. But when I did mess up, I'd beat myself up over it. I'd relive the moment, wondering what I could've done differently. This toxic mindset followed me into my adult life, affecting my relationships and overall well-being.

Self-sabotage became my defense mechanism—fueled by fear of failure and the belief that any mistake confirms my worst fear. Over time, this behavior took a tool on my mental health, allowing anxiety and depression to settle in. I felt being stuck under the weight of guilt and shame, not knowing how to release it or how to begin the process of self-forgiveness and healing.

One of the most profound moments that can change everything often comes during a simple, honest conversation. That moment happened to me while speaking with a close friend. In a moment of vulnerability, I broke down, sharing my struggles and fears. My friend listened without judgment, offering words of encouragement and understanding. In that moment, it became clear I was not alone.

That realization sparked a newfound sense of compassion. I began to see that I had been doing the best I could with the resources available at the time. This shift led to the practice of self-empathy—treating myself with the same kindness and understanding I would offer a close friend. It wasn't easy.

However, slowly, the guilt and shame began to fade, replaced by the liberating power of self-forgiveness.

That moment was life changing. The suffocating weight of past mistakes began to lift. Breathing became easier. Living felt possible again. A sense of self-compassion and clarity replaced the burden of shame. Forgiveness brought with it a gentler, more patient relationship with me. It dissolved the chains of self-doubt and anxiety, making room for courage and growth. Self-forgiveness became a turning point—empowering me to live a more authentic, fulfilling life, free from the burdens of guilt and shame.

And this is how I did it and still do it often. There's a beautiful garden that has become a personal sanctuary, despite the noise and busyness of others enjoying their walks there. I have a favorite spot, known as the Enchanted Forest. I sit down on my favorite bench, mid-morning when the soft breeze caresses my skin and occasionally the sun-ray kisses my face.

A notebook is pulled out. A piece of paper torn. Today's date is written at the top. Then, a confession of what's being held against myself: for messing up when I knew better, for closing off my heart, for carrying pain too long, for all the mistakes, everything. And then, a declaration: I forgive myself for it all. In that moment of forgiveness, I write down—*I am clean. I am pure.* Because deep down, I know it's true. I read it aloud. I raise the letter to the sky and read it aloud—every regret, and every forgiveness spoken into the air.

I repeat this until it is not needed anymore. Then, the paper is folded, and I look up toward the branches of the enchanted forest. It becomes a sacred moment—offering all that I have been holding against myself to something greater. The paper is held gently, allowing it to serve its purpose. To carry away what no longer needs to be carried. So that life can be lived as it was truly meant to be. After all, it's often the things held against the self that weigh more than anything else.

When the moment feels right, the paper is shredded into a thousand pieces and released into the wind—carried away bit by bit.

The paper came from nature, and it returns to it. I breathe in love that surrounds me, and I breathe out forgiveness.

And with the sharing of this story, may you gain a deeper insight into the quiet, transformative power of self-forgiveness. Now that your heart has opened to the possibility of letting go, step gently into the guided meditation. Let it hold your hand through the process of releasing pain, reclaiming peace, and forgiving — for your own freedom and true healing.

CHAPTER SIX

The Power of Self Love

This chapter is dedicated to anyone who has ever doubted their worth, struggled with self-criticism, or felt lost in the complexity of their own mind. It's for the young adult questioning identity, the overwhelmed professional facing burnout, the individual working through the aftermath of trauma, and anyone longing for a deeper, more compassionate relationship with themselves.

The journey toward self-love is a testament to one's inherent strength, resilience, and boundless capacity for growth. It's a commitment to quieting the whispers of self-doubt, embracing the roar of self-compassion, and cultivating the courage to grow. Evolve into this journey—for the destination is a life well-lived, a life brimming with the enduring power of self-love.

Self-care is not the same as self-love, though it plays an important role in achieving true self-love. The concept of self-love is not just a buzzword or a trendy idea—it's a vital part of overall well-being that can make a significant difference in one's life.

People must learn to love themselves as if their lives depend on it. When self-love is prioritized, individuals tend to become more confident, more resilient, and more genuinely happy. They show greater compassion toward themselves and others, and they are more likely to take risks, pursue passions, and live life to the fullest.

In a world constantly bombarded with messages suggesting inadequacy, it's easy to become overwhelmed by negativity and forget to prioritize personal well-being. But the truth is this: loving oneself is one of the most powerful things a person can do for their mental, emotional, and physical health. It's not selfish—it's essential.

By focusing on building a positive relationship with self, one opens the door to a life of confidence, resilience, and authentic joy. It's necessary to break free from the chains of societal expectations and start living from within. Rather than seeking validation externally, individuals need to begin finding it internally. And above all, it's necessary to start being unapologetically authentic—without fear of judgment or rejection.

Many people struggle to love themselves because they've been conditioned to believe they're not worthy. Societal pressures promote the idea that one must look a certain way, earn a certain income, or reach a specific status to deserve love and respect. When these arbitrary standards aren't met, it often leaves people feeling inadequate. It's a vicious cycle—one that can lead to overwhelming self-doubt and anxiety.

Many individuals feel stuck—trapped in a path of negativity, self-doubt, and mediocrity. There's a desire to break free, yet fears, insecurities, and limiting beliefs often hold them back. But what if that voice of self-doubt could be quieted? What if inner strength, resilience, and determination could be tapped into?

What if it were possible to reprogram the mind, the thoughts, and the beliefs—and witness a personal transformation unfold? The possibilities are endless. But what does self-love truly look like in practice? And how can it be incorporated into everyday life?

One of the biggest challenges people face when it comes to self-love is the tendency to prioritize others first. Family, friends, work—even social media—often take precedence over personal needs and desires. Lives are sacrificed for convenience, productivity, or the need to please others. Before long, the result is exhaustion, emptiness, and confusion over the source of such unhappiness.

Why, then, is it so difficult to love oneself? For many, the harshest critic lives within. Minor mistakes are magnified, and shortcomings are replayed on a loop. Negative self-talk becomes a major barrier to self-love. Constantly reinforcing the belief of "not being good enough" makes it incredibly hard to overcome feelings of inadequacy. Adding to the struggle is society's pressure to conform to standards of beauty, success, and perfection. People are bombarded with airbrushed images, curated lifestyles, and picture-perfect relationships. This often leads to the painful illusion that they simply don't measure up.

Many people often place others' opinions above their own, trying to please everyone else while abandoning their own needs and desires. Additionally, past experiences with trauma, abuse, or neglect can lead to deep-seated feelings of shame or unworthiness. There's also the fear of appearing selfish or self-indulgent—after all, society often teaches that putting others first is the ultimate virtue. But what about the idea of prioritizing oneself, even just for a change?

Individuals are often their own worst critics, beating themselves up over minor mistakes, dwelling on perceived flaws, and listening to that persistent inner voice whispering that they're not good enough. Then there's the pressure to conform to societal norms and beauty standards, the fear of being vulnerable or authentic, and the constant shortage of time and energy to focus on personal needs.

When someone becomes trapped in a cycle of negative self-talk, breaking free can feel impossible. The internal narrative shifts, and they begin to believe harmful lies—that they're too fat, too thin, too short, too stupid, too hyper, or too weak. Over time, these falsehoods become the story they tell themselves. They start to see only flaws and unworthiness, leading to self-doubt, diminished confidence, and even self-sabotage. It's a dangerous cycle, but importantly, it's one that can be broken.

The good news is that the narrative can be changed. It's possible to focus on personal strengths, celebrate small victories, and practice self-compassion. It may not be easy, but it's worth the effort. Every act of speaking kindly to oneself, recognizing achievements, and prioritizing well-being brings one step closer to breaking free from negativity and embracing the love and acceptance everyone deserves.

The negative voices in the mind can be quieted, making space for inner wisdom to surface. With time, it's possible to begin seeing oneself as truly worthy, deserving, and enough. And here's the truth: self-love isn't selfish—it's necessary. It's essential. And it begins with small, intentional choices made each day.

Following are eight meaningful self-love practices worth exploring. The first practice is to start a morning journaling routine. Spend 10 minutes each morning writing down thoughts, feelings, and moments of gratitude. This simple habit helps clear the mind, set intentions, and focus on daily goals.

The second practice is to schedule self-care Sundays. Set aside one day each week to unwind, reflect, and recharge. Whether it's applying a face mask, enjoying a long bath, or going for a solo hike, the key is to make the time meaningful and restorative. A personalized self-care routine should nourish the mind, body, and soul.

The third practice is to practice positive affirmations. These can be spoken aloud, written down, or displayed on a vision board. The important part is believing in one's own worth and potential. Daily affirmations such as "I am enough," "I am worthy of love and respect," or "I am beautiful inside and out" can help rewire the brain. Over time, they reinforce confidence, reduce limiting beliefs, and foster a more positive self-image.

The fourth practice is to set healthy boundaries. It's important to say no, establish limits, and prioritize personal well-being—without guilt. As the saying goes, one cannot pour from an empty cup. Setting boundaries allows individuals to let go of toxic relationships and make space for people who offer genuine support. For many, the hardest part is learning to say no—but doing so is essential to preserving emotional and mental health.

Saying "no," two little letters that can be incredibly difficult to utter. Many people have been there, stuck in situations that drain their energy and leave them feeling resentful, simply because they couldn't bring themselves to say no. But what if saying no is not only necessary—but liberating?

When faced with a request, the natural instinct is often to please others and agree to things one would rather not do. There's a fear that saying no will lead to conflict, hurt feelings, or damaged relationships. The worry is that others might think they're selfish or uncaring. And so, people find themselves overcommitting, spreading themselves too thin, and sacrificing their own needs and desires in the process. But what's the real cost of saying yes when no is what's truly meant? It's sanity, happiness, and well-being.

Consider the friend who always asks for favors, or the family member who assumes others will drop everything to help. Or the colleague who tries to pawn off their workload under the guise of "teamwork." These are all situations where saying no isn't just helpful—it's important. Yet many still struggle, fearing they'll be seen as uncooperative or unkind. But here's the truth: saying no to others often means saying yes to oneself—and that's a revolutionary concept.

Furthermore, saying yes out of obligation rather than genuine desire can lead to feelings of resentment and bitterness, which may slowly erode relationships and diminish self-worth. It can begin to feel like being trapped in a never-ending cycle of giving—without anyone ever asking what is needed in return. It's a difficult place to be in, but one that can be broken by mastering the art of saying no.

Saying no is not a selfish act, but a necessary one. Individuals need to prioritize their own needs and desires instead of constantly placing others first. This involves setting clear boundaries, communicating assertively, and being honest about limitations. It's not about being unkind—it's about staying authentic and respectful of one's own time and energy.

One effective strategy is the use of what can be called the *sandwich method*. This involves acknowledging the request, expressing gratitude for being considered, and then politely declining. For example: "Thank you so much for thinking of me for this project. I appreciate your trust in me, but there's a lot on my plate right now, and I don't think I can give it the attention it deserves." This approach helps maintain a positive relationship while still asserting individual needs.

Another strategy is to offer alternative solutions that work better for the individual. This shows a willingness to help—but on one's own terms. For instance: "I'd love to help you move this weekend, but I've got a prior commitment. How about I help you find someone else who might be available?" By doing so, a person takes control of the situation and prioritizes their own needs—without feeling guilty or apologetic.

Here's a personal story that illustrates this shift in mind-set. There was a time in my life when I constantly put other's needs ahead of my own, believing that love meant saying yes to everything no matter how ridiculous or inconvenient they were, even at the cost of my peace. I wore the label of "people-pleaser" like a badge of honor, but deep down, I was silently drowning in exhaustion and resentment.

Exhausted and stressed, I felt as if I was losing myself in the process. The turning point came when I hit a wall of burnout. I had given so much of myself away that there was barely anything left. In that still moment, I heard a truth rise within me: "NO" is not rejection—it is a form of self-respect. And it is a complete sentence.

From that moment forward, I began honoring my worth by setting healthy boundaries and prioritizing my own well-being. I stopped apologizing for choosing myself. And what I discovered was profound—my relationship with the right people grew stronger. Those who truly valued me began to mirror that respect. I no longer felt like I was losing myself to love others. Instead, I was loving from a place of fullness, not depletion which led to a renewed sense of confidence and control.

Saying no also revealed something deeper: those who took my refusal as selfish or unkind were never truly respectful of me or my time. That's when it became clear such individuals didn't just fail to deserve help; they didn't deserve a seat at my table at all.

Saying no without feeling guilty is not only possible but empowering. It's a declaration of self-love, self-respect, and self-care. When individuals learn to prioritize their own needs, they become happier, healthier, and more whole. So, the next time someone asks for something, take a deep breath, and say no without apology. Remember, it's okay to put oneself first sometimes.

The fifth practice is digital cleanse, to take breaks from social media. It's okay to disconnect, detox, and rediscover who one truly is outside of likes, comments, and followers. In today's digital age, it's easy to get sucked into the vortex of social media, email, and text notifications. But the truth is, all this constant stimulation can be draining on mental health. By setting aside device-free time each day, one can calm the mind, reduce anxiety, and recharge the energy.

Many people spend hours scrolling, tapping, and refreshing, losing track of time and missing out on real-life experiences.

It's time to take back control. Start by setting boundaries — such as designating specific times during the day to check your phone. This simple act can help one to reclaim those precious moments one has been wasting.

Next, try turning off notifications. Those little pings and alerts can be incredibly distracting. By silencing them, one will reduce the urge to check the phone constantly. Consider replacing screen time with activities that nourish the mind and body. One can go for a walk, read a book, or connect with friends face-to-face. It is amazing how rejuvenating these experiences can be. Breaking free from phone and social media addiction is a journey, not a sprint. Start small, be patient, and celebrate the progress.

The sixth ritual is all about movement. Whether it's a walk around the block, a yoga practice, or a high-intensity workout, moving the body is essential to releasing endorphins and boosting mood. The key is to find a type of movement that feels enjoyable, so it doesn't become a chore. By incorporating physical activity into a daily routine, individuals may begin to notice a significant shift in their energy and overall well-being.

Making exercise a daily habit is crucial for overall health and wellness. It's something most people know they *should* be doing but often struggle to fit into their busy lives. Yet the benefits are undeniable—regular exercise can improve mood, increase energy levels, and even add years to one's lifespan. So why is it so difficult to make it a priority?

One of the biggest challenges people face when trying to exercise regularly is finding the time. Many are busy juggling work, family, and social commitments, and it's easy for exercise to fall by the wayside. Another common obstacle is a lack of motivation. It can be tough to feel excited about hitting the gym when tired, stressed, or simply unmotivated. And the truth is, getting started is often the hardest part. Some may feel self-conscious about their bodies or unsure of what type of exercise suits them best.

Many people start strong, resolving to exercise every day, but then life gets in the way, and old habits return. Discouragement may set in due to a lack of visible progress, or it might start to feel like they're simply not cut out for consistent exercise. Then there's the fear of failure—what if they can't stick to their goals, or worse, get injured?

So how can these challenges be overcome to make exercise a daily habit? The key is to set realistic goals and start small. Instead of committing to an hour-long workout right away, beginning with just 10 or 15 minutes a day can be far more sustainable. Choosing an enjoyable activity—whether it's walking, jogging, yoga, or dancing—and making it a non-negotiable part of the daily routine can make a huge difference.

One of the most effective strategies for building a habit is to create an *implementation intention*. This is a specific plan for when and where the exercise will happen, along with strategies for overcoming potential obstacles. For example, someone might choose to work out first thing in the morning or right after dinner. Finding a workout buddy or accountability partner can also be a great motivator.

For many, the key to making exercise a habit lies in finding an activity they genuinely enjoy. When exercise doesn't feel like a chore, it becomes easier to stick with it. For some, that might be a brisk walk in nature—something that provides a sense of freedom and empowerment and can be done almost anywhere.

There will always be days when quitting feels tempting. With persistence and consistency, however, it's possible to turn exercise into a lasting habit. The rewards are well worth it: increased energy, better sleep, and a stronger sense of confidence.

The seventh practice is to practice self-compassion—treating oneself with kindness, understanding, and patience, just as one would treat a close friend. Mindfulness practices, such as meditation or yoga, can also support staying present and focused on the here and now, rather than getting caught up in negative thoughts or self-doubt. And it's important to celebrate the wins, no matter how small they may seem.

Finally, one particularly transformative practice is writing love letters to oneself. It might sound corny at first, but it can truly be a game-changer. Taking the time to acknowledge one's strengths, accomplishments, and growth helps shift focus from what's lacking to what's deeply appreciated. With this shift, a person begins to see themselves as capable, deserving, and worthy of love and respect. That shift in perspective—celebrating oneself, flaws and all—can be incredibly powerful.

Incorporating these self-care rituals into a daily routine may seem unfamiliar at first. Many start out skeptical, especially when feeling stuck, anxious, or overwhelmed. But as self-prioritization becomes more consistent, subtle yet profound changes begin to emerge. There's a growing sense of being more grounded, more centered, and more at peace. And it's not just about the rituals—it's the self-love and self-care that come along with them.

Looking back at my own progress of self-love, it became clear that these rituals weren't just about boosting mood—they were about transforming an entire approach to life. They served as reminders to slow down, stay present, and prioritize personal needs. And they have the potential to do the same for anyone. The key is to start small, start slow, and start now. There's no need to wait for the "perfect" moment or to feel completely "ready." Every individual is worthy of love, care, and compassion—just as they are, right now. When these practices come together, they create something powerful.

Here's my story that illustrates the importance of self-love. During a difficult breakup a few years ago, there was a sense of feeling lost and loneliness. It became evident that validation and love had been sought from outside sources, instead of being cultivated from within myself. It was a hard truth to accept, but it sparked a focus on my personal healing and growth.

Self-compassion became a priority, along with doing things that brought joy and caring for both my physical and mental health. It wasn't easy, but slowly, self-acceptance began to grow. I began to fall in love with myself—flaws and all.

Self-love is a journey; it isn't something that happens overnight; it's something to work toward every single day. There will be triumphs, and there will be setbacks. Some days will feel victorious, while others might feel like starting over. And that's okay. The important thing is to keep moving forward—to continue choosing self-love, even when it's hard.

Here's the thing: self-love is not a one-time achievement — it's a lifelong process. It's a path filled with ups and downs, twists and turns, triumphs and tears. But it's worth it. Choosing self-love opens the door to genuine happiness, confidence, and fulfillment. It encourages individuals to stop playing small, to stop apologizing for existing, and to begin living the life they truly deserve. Self-love isn't selfish—it's required. It's okay to prioritize personal needs and desires, and to focus on individual happiness and growth. Everyone is worthy of love and respect — and it begins from within.

Self-love is a continuous process of growth, self-discovery, and unwavering commitment to personal well-being. Embracing the journey and celebrating progress, while recognizing that each person is worthy of love and acceptance just as they are, is vital. The path may have its twists and turns, but the destination — a life filled with self-compassion and joy — is well worth the effort.

By consistently implementing these practices, a strong foundation of self-love can be built — one that sustains a person throughout life. This isn't just about feeling good; it's about cultivating a life that is genuinely fulfilling, authentic, and aligned with deeply held values. Continue nurturing the inner garden of self-love — the rewards are immeasurable.

This chapter was a love letter to your soul. The meditation that follows is your invitation to turn inward, soften your heart, and begin — or deepen — the lifelong journey of loving yourself like your life depends on it. Because it does.

Part Three:
Elevate-Let it Come

Now that the journey of embracing true identity has been taken by walking down the memory lane of the past and evolving into a stronger, more authentic version of self, it's time to live fully and leave a legacy for generations to come.

Living life to the fullest is a concept that resonates with many. It's about embracing each moment, seizing opportunities, and making the most of the life given. It's important to consider a life marked by abundance, courage, gratitude, and purpose. Ultimately, living fully is a conscious choice — a decision to take action, face risks, and build a life that genuinely reflects one's values and aspirations.

As you step into this next season of elevation, let the words you've just read settle into your heart. You've done the soul work—now allow your spirit to rise. Take a deep breath, quiet your mind, and prepare to enter a sacred space of stillness. In this guided meditation, you'll be invited to visualize the life you're meant to live—bold, abundant, and anchored in purpose. Let this moment be your bridge from inspiration to transformation. Elevate, immerse, and let it come.

CHAPTER SEVEN

A Life of Abundance and Prosperity

This chapter is dedicated to every individual who has ever dared to dream of a life beyond their current circumstances; to those who have felt the weight of limiting beliefs and still found the courage to challenge themselves; to the unwavering spirits who seek not just financial wealth, but a holistic abundance that includes joy, health, fulfilling relationships, and a profound sense of purpose.

Manifesting abundance and prosperity are within reach for everyone. The power to shape a meaningful life already exists within. It begins with the mindset. When rooted in positivity, kindness, compassion, and gratitude, that mindset creates a ripple effect that leads to a meaningful and purposeful life.

Living abundantly isn't simply about acquiring money or possessions. It's about a life rich in experiences, deep connections, and personal growth. It's about waking each morning with gratitude, inspiration, and a sense of fulfillment. This is the key to unlocking true potential and living a life that stands out as truly remarkable.

Many people get stuck in the belief that abundance is something they'll experience someday after reaching a certain level of success or hitting a specific milestone. In reality, abundance is available in the present moment. There's no need to wait. It's possible to choose to live abundantly right now, regardless of current circumstances.

There's also a common misconception that abundance is reserved for a select few for those who are lucky or exceptionally talented. But abundance is a mindset that anyone can embrace. It's a daily choice, not defined by external achievements, but by living a life that aligns with one's true self and deepest desires.

Living abundantly begins with gratitude. Focusing on what one is thankful for shifts energy and attention toward what is already present, rather than what is missing. This practice encourages appreciation for small things to find joy in the everyday moments, and to cultivate a sense of fulfillment, no matter what circumstances are.

People often underestimate the power of individual actions, and that's exactly what prevents many from taking the first step toward gratitude. It's important to shift the mindset and begin to see oneself as an agent of change. Practicing gratitude nurtures a sense of purpose and fulfillment. Every single act of gratefulness, no matter how small, holds the potential to create a ripple effect that spreads far and wide.

At the same time, it's important to release the belief that abundance is only about gaining more. True abundance can also mean letting go of what holds one back or no longer serves the individual. It's about making room for new experiences, relationships, and opportunities to enter lives. It's about welcoming a new beginning and a fresh start.

A fresh start—two words that can be both exhilarating and intimidating—holds the power to transform a life in ways once thought impossible. It can lead to personal growth, self-discovery, and a renewed sense of purpose.

One of the biggest obstacles that holds people back from initiating a fresh start is fear—of the unknown, of failure, of being alone, or even the fear of success. Many get stuck in their comfort zones, even when those spaces no longer serve them, simply because they're familiar and easy. But staying in a place of stagnation often leads to regret, sadness, and frustration—early signs that can spiral into depression. When someone is stuck, moving forward and personal growth become nearly impossible.

Another barrier to abundant living is the weight of negative thinking. It's easy to fall into a scarcity mindset, constantly focusing on what's missing, what's lacking, or what's going wrong. This kind of thinking quietly holds people back, making it harder to access their full potential. And the worst part is, it's often unconscious.

Past failures can also keep individuals from taking that first step toward a fresh start. Feelings of not being good enough, smart enough, or capable enough can become paralyzing. The cycle of self-doubt and negativity is powerful, but here's the truth: the past doesn't define anyone. There is always the power to learn from mistakes, grow through them, and move forward.

There was a time in my life that I was in a relationship that was draining every ounce of my energy. I stayed in because I was afraid of being alone, an emotion that was instilled in me from childhood. I truly felt and believed that if I am ever alone that means I am not worthy of love, and the price I paid for that conditional love and temporary lust was paid with my entire soul and my entire being. That went on for a very long time, till I decided enough is enough and it is time to change and here I am, proudly transformed.

Stepping out of the comfort zone can be one of the hardest things to do. But with a little perseverance and a whole lot of faith, the rewards are truly priceless. Hearts begin to heal, souls feel free, and one can breathe again. There's no more walking on eggshells, no more seeking acceptance from others.

So, how does someone begin to make progress toward a fresh start? One key strategy is to set clear, achievable goals. These goals should be specific, measurable, and aligned with personal values and long-term aspirations. Having a clear sense of direction helps maintain focus and motivation, even when the journey becomes challenging.

It's also essential to cultivate a positive mindset. Focusing on negativity tends to attract more of it, often leading to a path of self-doubt and fear. But choosing to focus on the positive allows individuals to tap into inner strength, resilience, and determination. Challenges can be reframed as opportunities, and even difficult situations can reveal hidden treasures.

Having the right mindset is crucial in creating the life many dream of. In today's fast-paced world, thoughts and beliefs play a significant role in shaping reality. It's easy to get swept up in the demands of daily life. Without awareness, mindset alone can become a barrier to reaching full potential.

There are many different techniques and practices that can help shift a person's mindset. One of the most powerful is the use of affirmations. Affirmations are simple yet impactful statements that help rewire the brain and reshape thought patterns. They act as a daily dose of positivity, directing focus toward desired outcomes. For instance, someone struggling with low confidence might use the affirmation, "I am capable and confident in everything I do." Repeating this daily trains the brain to believe it.

Another effective technique is visualization. This is a powerful tool for reprogramming the subconscious mind and turning dreams into reality. It functions like a mental rehearsal, vividly imagining the achievement of goals and the triumph over challenges. It's as if one is watching a personal movie on a giant cinema screen—only they are the star of that story.

Gratitude is also a deeply transformative practice for shifting mindset. When individuals focus on what they're thankful for, they begin to attract more positivity into their lives. They start noticing the good in situations and appreciating what they already have. The practice is simple yet profoundly effective. Taking just a few minutes each day to jot down three things to be grateful for—even something as small as a warm cup of coffee or a bright sunny morning—can make a meaningful difference. The key is to focus on these moments and begin recognizing the good that already exists.

Reaching one's highest potential is a common aspiration, yet it often feels like a distant dream. Many desire to become the best version of themselves, to accomplish meaningful goals, and to live a truly fulfilling life. But it's not only about wanting these things — it's about taking consistent action to bring them to life. One essential step in that journey is raising the vibrational frequency from a mindset of lack to one of abundance.

A fresh start is powerful. A few years ago, I found myself feeling stuck—lost in the noise of uncertainty and unsure of what the future held. Deep down, I knew something had to shift, even if I didn't yet know how. I surrendered to the unknown and began with small, intentional steps to raise my vibrational energy.

I started rising with the sun, moving my body with purpose, and immersing myself in words that uplifted my spirit. Over time, those small shifts created momentum, and with that came the clarity and courage to pursue my passion and begin again—with purpose and power.

Elevating one's vibrational frequency involves shifting daily habits and thought patterns while making conscious choices that support well-being and positivity. This journey can begin with simple, actionable steps that are easy to incorporate into everyday life.

Cultivating positive thoughts is critical. Thoughts have a powerful impact on vibrational frequency. Each thought carries energy that can either uplift or lower an individual's overall vibration. Shifting toward positive thinking is one of the most effective ways to elevate this frequency. It involves acknowledging low-frequency thoughts while consciously focusing on more uplifting perspectives.

There are generally two types of vibrational energy: contracted energy and expanded energy. Contracted or depleted energy stems from emotions like shame, guilt, apathy, grief, fear, desire, anger, and pride. Expanded or higher energy, on the other hand, arises from acceptance, reason, love, joy, peace, and ultimately enlightenment. The more one moves from shame toward love, the higher the vibrational energy and frequency become—in other words, shifting from negative emotions to more positive ones.

Gratitude is a key habit to develop in order to raise your vibrational energy. Taking a moment each day to reflect on or write down things to be thankful for can naturally redirect focus to the positive areas of life. Visualization is also a helpful practice. Envisioning positive outcomes and experiences uplifts the mood and helps align the subconscious mind with a higher frequency. Engaging with books, podcasts, and conversations that encourage optimism, and personal development reinforces the commitment to maintaining a positive mindset.

Nourish the body wisely. The food consumed daily plays a significant role in influencing vibrational frequency. High-vibrational foods are alive and full of natural energy. This includes fresh fruits and vegetables, which are rich in essential nutrients and carry life energy from the sun and earth. Incorporating these wholesome foods into a daily diet introduces vibrant, natural energy into the body, helping to raise overall vibrational frequency.

Such foods are typically less processed and free from additives, retaining their natural integrity and energetic qualities. Foods like organic greens, ripe fruits, nuts, and seeds are loaded with vitamins, minerals, and antioxidants that nourish the body and support a clearer, more positive state of mind. Drinking plenty of water especially when purified or naturally sourced—is also crucial for maintaining a high vibration. Water supports life and helps flush out toxins, keeping the body's energy flowing clearly and vibrantly.

In contrast, heavily processed foods, excess sugars, and artificial additives tend to carry lower vibrational frequencies. These can contribute to feelings of sluggishness or negativity, as they are harder for the body to digest and lack vital nutrients. Choosing high-vibrational foods supports physical health while fostering a more elevated energetic state. With consistent, mindful dietary choices, many notice increased energy, improved mental clarity, and a deeper sense of wellbeing—reflecting the higher vibrational energy being cultivated.

If you're ready to take the next step in nourishing your body and elevating your energy, I've created a free resource just for you. Whether you're just starting or looking to refine your routine, my downloadable diet plan (or free eBook) is packed with practical tips, sample meals, and high-vibrational food suggestions to support your wellness journey. Visit my website **www.RobiJulian.com** and grab your copy today—because when you fuel your body with intention, you empower your life with purpose.

Connecting with nature is essential. Nature offers an unparalleled source of high vibrational energy, and immersing in natural surroundings can be deeply uplifting. Time spent in nature provides exposure to life's pure, unfiltered essence. The natural world operates at a frequency that is calming and rejuvenating. Whether it's the serene stillness of a forest, the gentle rhythm of waves on a beach, or the tranquil beauty of a mountain range, each setting carries a unique vibrational signature that supports realignment and elevates energy levels.

Engaging the senses fully. Feeling the breeze as it caresses the skin, listening to the rustle of leaves whispering sweetness into the ears, or watching the dance of light on water as waves crash into the shore, allows for a fuller absorption of the natural energy around us. This sensory interaction facilitates a deeper connection, harmonizing one's vibrations with the earth's natural rhythms. It becomes a process of grounding, where lower vibrational energies are released and replaced with the serene, vibrant energy of the natural world.

Spending time outdoors increases exposure to sunlight, which is essential for vitamin D production—a key factor in maintaining both physical and mental health. The benefits extend to improved mood, enhanced focus, and a greater sense of happiness and gratitude. Regularly setting aside time for nature becomes a conscious practice in aligning with a higher, more harmonious vibrational state. This connection gently reminds individual of the beauty and simplicity of life, encouraging a shift in perspective toward peace and positivity.

Regular exercise is a powerful tool for enhancing vibrational frequency. When the body engages in physical activity, it releases endorphins—commonly known as "feel-good" hormones. These natural mood lifters promote a sense of well-being and happiness. This biochemical shift improves mood and raises energetic vibration. Movement, whether through aerobic workouts, strength training, yoga, or even a simple walk, helps release stagnant energy and boost circulation—both essential for maintaining a high vibrational state.

Exercise also plays a vital role in reducing stress. By lowering levels of stress hormones such as adrenaline and cortisol, it encourages relaxation and calm, aligning the body with higher vibrational frequencies. Consistent physical activity can also clear mental clutter, allowing for greater focus and a more positive mindset.

The type of exercise chosen can influence vibration as well. Mindful activities like yoga or tai chi benefit both the physical and energetic body, helping to balance and align the chakras or energy centers. These practices often pair movement with deep, intentional breathing, further detoxifying and energizing the system. Even high-intensity workouts such as running or cycling can lead to a state often referred to as "runner's high," a euphoric feeling accompanied by reduced anxiety and increased emotional clarity, indicative of a heightened vibrational state.

Meditation is another important and highly recommended practice that involves quieting the mind, allowing for a deeper connection with the inner self and the present moment. This practice is essential for aligning one's energy with higher frequencies, fostering peace and clarity. Through meditation, individuals step away from the constant mental chatter—worries, plans, and distractions—and create space for their energy to shift from the fast pace of daily life to a more serene and elevated state.

The benefits of meditation extend well beyond the moments spent in practice. Over time, regular meditation increases mindfulness throughout the day. This heightened awareness helps individuals become more attuned to their thoughts and emotions, empowering them to consciously choose those that support a higher vibration. For example, they may recognize a negative thought pattern and intentionally redirect their focus toward more uplifting and positive thinking.

Meditation has also been shown to reduce stress and anxiety—states often linked to lower vibrational frequencies. As these feelings diminish, the body and mind are able to relax and recharge, supporting an overall elevated state of being. Moreover, consistent meditation can enhance empathy and compassion, emotions that naturally resonate with higher vibrational energy.

Being surrounded by positive influence is key. The energy of the people and environments around an individual can significantly impact their vibrational frequency. Being in the presence of positive, supportive individuals influences mood, outlook, and overall emotional state. These people radiate energy rooted in optimism, encouragement, and joy, creating an atmosphere where higher vibrations can thrive.

The physical environment also plays a role in shaping vibrational frequency. Spaces that are bright, clean, and filled with natural elements such as plants or sunlight tend to promote more positive and elevated energy. In contrast, cluttered, dim, or chaotic spaces may contribute to lower vibrational energy. Simple changes—like organizing the living space, allowing in natural light, or incorporating elements of nature—can create a noticeable improvement.

The media and content consumed also influence vibrational well-being. Constant exposure to negative news, violent entertainment, or pessimistic social media can lower one's energy. Choosing uplifting, inspiring content aligned with personal values and goals makes a meaningful difference.

Motivational books, positive music, and educational podcasts are examples of sources that support higher vibrations. By consciously curating these influences, individuals actively support and elevate their vibrational frequency.

Another creative way is found in aromatherapy and color—subtle and yet powerful ways to influence vibrational state. Both aromatherapy and colors engage the senses in ways that directly connect to emotions and energy levels. Aromatherapy, which uses natural plant extracts typically essential oils can promote overall well-being.

Different scents offer different effects; for instance, lavender is known for its calming and relaxing properties, helping to reduce stress and elevate vibration. Citrus scents, such as orange or lemon, are recognized for their uplifting and energizing qualities. Incorporating these aromas into daily routines through diffusers, candles, or personal care products can help sustain a higher vibrational frequency.

Colors can impact mood and energy. They are light of varying wavelengths, and each color has a unique vibrational frequency. Bright, warm colors such as yellow, orange, and red are often associated with energy, joy, and vitality. In contrast, cooler tones like blue and green are linked to calmness, relaxation, and rejuvenation. Integrating these colors into the environment—through clothing, décor, or artwork—can help create a space that reflects the energy one wishes to cultivate.

Combining aromatherapy with color therapy can be especially effective. For example, using a lavender-scented candle in a room decorated with soothing blue tones can create a tranquil atmosphere, ideal for meditation and relaxation. Conversely, a citrus-scented diffuser in a brightly colored space can energize and stimulate mental clarity. By staying mindful of the sensory elements in a space, it becomes possible to create an environment that not only appeals to the senses but also supports the intention to maintain a high vibrational state.

Fostering gratitude and compassion is essential for enhancing vibrational frequency. These emotions reshape the internal landscape, shifting attention from lack or negativity to abundance and empathy.

Regular expressions of gratitude help acknowledge the positive aspects of life, no matter how small. This simple shift in focus naturally raises one's vibration, attracting more positivity and contentment. Keeping a gratitude journal, noting daily moments of thankfulness, reinforces awareness of life's blessings and supports a consistently elevated state of being.

Compassion involves extending kindness and understanding to others, regardless of their circumstances. Practicing compassion nurtures deeper human connection and fosters feelings of love and empathy. These emotions resonate at higher frequencies, contributing to a sense of unity and collective well-being.

Acts of compassion may range from small gestures of kindness to more meaningful contributions such as charity or volunteer work. Each act not only benefits the recipient but also uplifts the giver's vibrational state.

Engaging in practices that develop both gratitude and compassion can significantly impact emotional health. These practices help reduce stress, anxiety, and depression—emotions typically associated with lower vibrational states. By cultivating gratitude and compassion, individuals not only enhance their own emotional well-being but also contribute to a more positive and empathetic world.

There was a time in my life of deep struggle with anxiety and depression—a period marked by a pattern of negativity that felt impossible to escape. But everything began to shift with one simple practice: daily gratitude. I started focusing on good things in my life, and slowly but surely, my mindset started to shift. I started to see the world in a different light, and I started to believe in myself again. It was an incredible transformation and a powerful example of how mindset can shape reality.

Of course, shifting one's mindset takes time and effort, but it's worth it. The power to create a fulfilling life lies within, and it all begins with thoughts and beliefs. Looking back, those small, consistent steps became the foundation for total transformation in my life. I learned to believe in myself, to take risks, and to trust that everything would work out for my highest good. I learned how to rewire my brain, how to shift my mindset, and how to focus on what I wanted, rather than what I didn't want. And it was life changing— a new way of seeing the world, a renewed sense of self-belief, and a life aligned with true identity.

What I learned from that experience is that abundance is not just about achieving some kind of external success, it's about living a life that's true to who I am. It's about authentic-ity, it's about vulnerability, and it's about embracing myself— without apology.

The focus should be on progress, not perfection. It's important to be kind to oneself, to celebrate wins, and to learn from failures. Positive affirmations, gratitude, and a healthy lifestyle are all incredibly powerful tools. When individuals repeat affirmations, express gratitude for what they have and what's to come, and commit to a vibrant life, their mindset begins to shift.

Individuals start to see themselves in a new light—as capable and strong. Consider this: what would life look like if lived at the highest potential? What could be achieved? What would it feel like? Take a moment to truly imagine it. Feel it. Then take action. One step today can begin to make that vision a reality. Reaching one's highest potential is a path worth taking. Let this serve as a daily reminder: abundance is a choice. It's a choice that can be made every morning, every moment. There's always the option to focus on what's missing, but there's also the power to focus on what's present. One can choose a life of scarcity, or a life filled with abundance and prosperity.

You are meant to live in overflow. As you move into the next meditation, allow yourself to feel worthy of abundance — not someday, but now. Let this be your moment to align with the richness already available to you.

CHAPTER EIGHT

A Life of Bold Courage

This chapter is dedicated to every individual who has ever felt the weight of societal expectations, the sting of self-doubt, or the fear of stepping outside their comfort zone. It is for those who have silenced their inner voice to conform to unrealistic standards, sacrificing passions and dreams on the altar of external validation.

These pages are a testament to the strength within, the unwavering spirit, and the incredible potential each person holds. They are a celebration of the courage that already exists, the courage waiting to be unleashed. And to the bold and beautiful life that lies ahead. These pages highlight the power of self-belief and serve as a reminder that worth is not defined by outside approval, but by the unwavering strength of the heart and the lasting impact left on the world. Dare to be different. Dare to be authentic.

In a world saturated with curated perfection, where social media rules and the pressure to conform is relentless, it is easy to lose sight of one's true self. Individuals are constantly bombarded with unrealistic standards, leaving many feeling inadequate, lost, and suffocated.

This is a personal invitation to embark on a transformative journey of self-discovery. It's a call to action, urging all to break free from the shackles of societal pressures and embrace the extraordinary individuals born to be.

This is a journey of self-discovery shaped by the ability to be courageous, the willingness to take risks, to be bold, and to step outside the comfort zone. In a world where social media reigns supreme, it's easy to get caught up in the idea that certain standards must be followed to be accepted, to be loved, and to live fully.

Elevating to a continuous growth is not merely a desirable trait; it is the very essence of a life lived authentically and boldly. The journey of self-discovery is not another path, but an ongoing process of unfolding, learning, and adapting. It is a lifelong adventure filled with both exhilarating highs and challenging lows, where the most meaningful growth often emerges from navigating the complexities of life's unexpected turns.

Being bold is not just about making reckless decisions or taking unnecessary risks. It means living fully, seizing each opportunity, and making the most of every moment. Boldness invites new experiences, new relationships, and new possibilities. It reflects a decision to take control of life and begin creating the lifelong envisioned.

Courage is what sets individuals free from the chains of fear and doubt. It allows a person to live a life of purpose and meaning — a life that is true to who they are. Without courage, many remain stuck in their comfort zones, too afraid to take the leap and make meaningful changes. To experience true fulfillment and contentment, one must be courageous enough to take a chance and embrace change.

Courage is the spark that ignites the fire of transformation. It serves as the catalyst that turns deep desires into reality. Without it, life can become mundane, filled with hesitation and missed opportunities. But choosing courage opens the door to a world of possibilities.

There are many types of courage, each essential in its own way. Emotional courage, for example, enables individuals to be vulnerable and honest with their feelings. It is the willingness to experience discomfort, to face unpleasant emotions, and to act in alignment with personal values. It's about following the heart and intuition, even when it's difficult, rather than choosing what feels safe or familiar.

Emotional courage is what allows a person to be honest with themselves and others, to admit their fears and doubts, and to be willing to work through them. It's the strength behind saying "I'm not okay" when struggling, acknowledging weaknesses, and asking for help when needed. But admitting is only half of the battle—working to resolve it is the other half.

During my teenage years, I struggled to communicate my emotions. This often led to emotional suppression and using feelings interchangeably to avoid facing the truth. Yet, that challenge became a hidden gift. I discovered a way to channel those emotions into written words and lose myself in the fascinating world of imagination. As a young woman who faced difficulties at school because English wasn't my first language, that discovery was its own kind of courage.

Social courage is another that gives individuals the strength to speak their truth and stand up for what they believe in. It's about standing tall, meeting the world with confidence, and feeling at ease in one's own skin. I am a living proof of that. Despite cultural norms, I chose to leave a relationship that no longer served me—relationship that held me back instead of allowing me to grow.

Social courage means not conforming to the expectations of others—being willing to show one's true self, even if it risks social disapproval or judgment. It involves expressing opinions and preferences without needing to align with what "everyone else" thinks. This kind of courage is what guided me to step away from certain people and environments that were quietly eroding my soul and spirit, choosing instead to be alone and rediscover my own authenticity.

Social courage gives individuals the strength to take a stand, speak honestly, and be unapologetically themselves. It empowers people to set boundaries, say "no" when necessary, and stay true to personal values. It means saying no to destructive patterns and yes to intuition and inner truth—embracing new possibilities while letting go of the past.

Physical courage, on the other hand, is what drives a person to face fear and uncertainty. It encourages risk-taking and personal challenge. It's shown in the willingness to try new things and to confront discomfort or danger with resilience. Physical courage involves not just bravery, when they face fear, pain, uncertainty, or danger, but the development of physical strength, awareness, and the ability to endure hardship.

A while back, I was diagnosed with Hashimoto's thyroiditis—an autoimmune disease that gradually destroys the thyroid gland. I had two choices, let it consume me, or I fight back. And by now, it's clear which path was chosen. Everything happening at that time seemed to point toward surrender. But there was a greater purpose, and taking care of my physical needs became essential in order to be well enough to share my story.

It became one of the most empowering experiences imaginable. It revealed an inner strength that I hadn't been fully recognized it before—the ability to overcome obstacles, to take risks, and to grow through adversity. That journey proved that with one bold first step, anything was possible. It uncovered the power of embracing my uniqueness and my personal strength. It took courage to be bold, to take a stand, and to remain authentic no matter the circumstances. And from that place of growth came the desire to inspire others to do the same.

I was ridiculed for the dramatic lifestyle change—the diet, the meditation, the exercise, the consistent sleep routine. These choices didn't align with my partner at the time, but that didn't stop me. The decision was to live fully, without clinging to comforts that no longer supported my healing. That choice marked a bold shift, especially for someone who had always tried to please others. But enough was enough—it was time to stand up for what was right.

Everyone has different reasons that hold them back from flourishing and elevating to their highest potential. Many feel trapped in a never-ending race filled with competition and a sense of disconnect. But now is the time to break free from those chains and embrace one's true self, imperfections and all. Being bold and celebrating unique individuality is vital in today's world, where it's easy to get lost in the sea of sameness.

Choosing to be bold and different often comes with many challenges. Stepping outside of the comfort zone brings uncertainty. The unknown can be frightening, and that fear can be paralyzing. It causes many to play it safe and hide their authentic selves. But fear is a natural part of being human, and while it's valid, it should not be the reason bold changes are avoided.

Fear of failure, rejection, and uncertainty is common. People often worry about what others might think. They doubt their worth, question their ability to succeed, and hesitate to take risks. There is fear of being judged, of making mistakes, and of not being able to bounce back. The thought of losing sense of familiarity and stability can be overwhelming, even when that false security is suffocating. And perhaps most daunting of all, there is fear of having to begin anew.

But the truth is, these fears are just illusions. They are mere shadows of what could be, and they hold many people back from living the life they truly want. Often, individuals are limited by their own beliefs—another subtle form of fear. They tell themselves they're not strong enough, not talented enough, or not worthy. It's important to recognize that these beliefs are untrue and that each person has the power to overcome them.

So how can these challenges be overcome? It begins with self-reflection. The topic that has been mentioned in almost every chapter. In the simplest form, self-reflection means taking the time to understand what drives someone, what they stand for, and what makes them unique. It's not always easy, but it's worth the effort.

Inspiration can also come from those who have boldly gone against the grain. Consider people like Lady Gaga, who has never been afraid to speak her mind or be herself, regardless of what others think. Or Steve Jobs, who revolutionized the tech industry through innovative thinking and a fearless approach to design.

Their stories are a testament to the strength found in embracing individuality. They remind people that being different isn't something to fear—it's something to take pride in. When people celebrate what sets them apart, they open themselves to new experiences, meaningful connections, and a deeper understanding of who they are.

When individuals try to fit in, they risk losing themselves in the process. They begin comparing themselves to others, and that's when self-doubt starts to creep in. They begin to question their own worth, and that's a dangerous game to play. The truth is nobody is perfect. Everyone has flaws, and that's what makes each person unique and beautiful.

It takes courage to be different, to embrace imperfections, and to celebrate one's uniqueness. Many people become so accustomed to daily routines and comfortable lives that they forget what it's like to truly feel alive. The only way to break free from that cycle is by taking risks, stepping outside of comfort zones, and challenging oneself to be more, do more, and achieve more.

There's a common tendency to say, "I'll take a risk when I'm ready," or "I'll take a risk when the time is right." But the truth is, there is no perfect time, and no perfect way to be ready. The only way forward is to take that leap of faith—to trust oneself and trust the journey.

One of the most pivotal moments in my life was deciding to leave the business that I built over the years and pursue my passion for writing. It was a frightening decision, one filled with fear and uncertainty. But it had to be done—a chance had to be taken on my personal growth and creative abilities. And it was one of the best decisions I've ever made. It taught me that I had the courage to take risks, to challenge myself, and to pursue my dreams, no matter how intimidating it might seem.

Taking a risk to begin writing was terrifying and difficult, and there were many moments filled with self-doubt. Yet, it became one of the best decisions I ever made. It created space to pursue my passion, live on my own terms, and fully embrace my authenticity.

There are countless examples of people who have taken bold risks and achieved extraordinary things—those who left their jobs to explore the world, founded non-profit organizations, or chased dreams others labeled unrealistic. In every case, their lives experienced profound transformation.

Risk opens the door to growth, learning, and personal evolution. These elements are essential to becoming the best version of oneself. Fear doesn't need to hold anyone back from stepping outside their comfort zone and pursuing bold aspirations. When they do, however, the transformation can be incredible.

To begin this journey of boldness and adventure, the first step is to set clear goals. What is it one truly wants to achieve, accomplish, or create? With clarity of purpose, direction and motivation follow naturally. Focus shifts from fear to vision—and that shift changes everything.

The second step is to take calculated risks. This doesn't mean being reckless or impulsive. It means making informed decisions, weighing the pros and cons, and then taking that leap of faith. When calculated risks are taken, new opportunities and the right people often begin to appear. That is when true growth becomes visible.

The third step is to build a circle of people who inspire and motivate. Who are the individuals that push others to become their best selves? Who encourages boldness, risk-taking, and living fully? When surrounded by this kind of energy, confidence grows, inspiration deepens, and motivation becomes more natural.

The fourth step is to stay grounded in the present moment. Instead of worrying about the future or dwelling on the past, it's important to focus on what can be controlled—in this very moment. Living in the present helps individuals feel more centered, grounded, and connected to their true selves.

Looking back, taking bold steps one after another became some of the best decisions I ever made. Walking away from a toxic relationship, healing through nature, and sharing my personal story each led to deeper growth. These choices nurtured resilience, resourcefulness, and confidence. They created the space for a life that aligned with my authenticity, with who I AM.

One of the most powerful quotes comes from Oscar Wilde: "Be yourself, because an original is worth more than a copy." This quote resonates deeply, serving as a reminder that uniqueness is what sets each person apart and what makes them valuable. Embracing one's true self allows for a more authentic, fulfilling life. And this isn't just a personal truth. When individuality is celebrated, it inspires others to do the same. That creates a ripple effect of self-acceptance and empowerment across communities and generations.

Steve Jobs once expressed a similar sentiment: "Remembering that I'll be dead soon is the most important tool I've ever encountered to help me make the big choices in life." This perspective reminds us that time is limited. That awareness makes it more likely to take bold steps, pursue passions, and live life intentionally. Ultimately, it's not only about the risks taken—it's about who one becomes in the process. Growth comes from stepping outside comfort zones, challenging limits, and pursuing dreams with courage.

The journey of self-discovery requires a commitment to lifelong learning. It's about expanding horizons, questioning assumptions, and welcoming new experiences. It involves engaging with different perspectives and continuously seeking understanding. This kind of learning isn't confined to degrees or certifications; it's rooted in curiosity—a mindset that touches every part of life.

Cultivating resilience is essential in the journey of growth. Life is unpredictable — it throws curveballs, unexpected challenges, and setbacks that can test one's limits. Developing resilience means learning to bounce back from adversity, adapt to change, and maintain a positive outlook in the face of difficulty. It takes courage and boldness to build that resilience and to overcome setbacks with strength and grace.

Remember, the path of self-discovery is unique for every individual. There is no right or wrong way to live boldly and authentically. Embracing individuality, celebrating strengths, and acknowledging imperfections are key. The path to self-discovery is deeply personal, and it's through accepting the sum of one's strengths and vulnerabilities that true growth and elevation takes place.

Here's a challenge worth considering: What's one bold step that can be taken today? What's one risk that might lead closer to a desired life? What's one decision that could move things forward in a meaningful way? This is an invitation to act, be bold, and honor what makes each person unique. Take that step, embrace that risk, and trust the leap of faith—it might just lead to something extraordinary.

Embrace the continuous journey for it is in the constant striving, the ongoing learning, and the unwavering commitment to growth that one discovers their truest, boldest self. This journey is personal and unique. Own it, nurture it, and embrace the transformative power of continuous growth. It is a journey worth taking and a life worth living.

You don't need permission to be powerful — but you do need to own it. The following meditation is a call to rise into boldness, silence fear, and let your courage lead the way. Take a breath and step into your strength.

CHAPTER NINE

A Life of Fulfillment

This chapter is dedicated to the countless individuals who have embarked on their own journeys of self-discovery and personal growth. It is for those who have sought meaning and purpose amidst the chaos of modern life—those who have dared to question societal norms and embrace their authentic selves.

It honors the dreamers, the seekers, and the quiet revolutionaries who strive to live each day with intention and awareness. This work stands as a testament to the resilience of the human spirit and the transformative power of mindfulness. It is dedicated to everyone who has ever felt lost, overwhelmed, or unfulfilled, yet found the courage to seek a path toward a more meaningful existence.

May these pages serve as a lighthouse—a gentle companion on the personal journey to a life filled with purpose, joy, and lasting contentment. May it be a reminder of the inherent beauty in the everyday, the power of presence, and the boundless potential that resides within each person. This is a dedication to the quiet moments of reflection, the courageous acts of self-compassion, and the enduring commitment to live a life truly aligned with the heart's deepest desires.

A life that aligns with personal values is a path that leads to happiness. There is so much beauty around, if only one takes the time to notice it. And when that happens, happiness is experienced. To truly feel happiness, it's important to train the mind to live in the present moment—to savor it for what it is, rather than constantly anticipating the future or dwelling on the past. Mastery of life comes only through the act of living it.

Happiness is something everyone strives for, yet it can sometimes feel like an impossible dream. But it isn't something to be found; it's something to be created. In this final chapter, the focus shifts to the concept of happiness, exploring different ways a person can begin living a more fulfilling life.

It's a familiar feeling—being stuck, stressed, overwhelmed, and simply unhappy. It can feel like trying to solve a puzzle with missing pieces. No matter the effort, something just doesn't click. Societal pressures often dictate the need to be successful, to earn a certain income, to have the perfect partner, to appear as though everything is in order. But what if that very pressure is contributing to unhappiness? What if the things believed to bring joy are actually what hold people back?

People are constantly bombarded with messages suggesting they're not good enough—that they need to be better, do more, and achieve more. It's exhausting. Over time, it becomes easy to believe that working harder, earning more, or accomplishing every goal will eventually lead to happiness. But the truth is, happiness doesn't come from external sources. It comes from within. And that's a hard pill to swallow, because it requires taking personal responsibility to create happiness.

Many have been conditioned to see happiness as a destination something to reach once everything falls into place. But what if happiness is not a destination at all? What if it's a process made up of small moments, daily choices, and intentional actions that invite joy along the way? That's the focus of this chapter.

The key to lasting happiness is gratitude. A very familiar and repetitive concept that was mentioned throughout the book. Gratitude is a powerful tool that draws positivity and abundance into life. It's about shifting focus from what's missing to what's already present and being thankful for it. When practiced consistently, gratitude leads to greater happiness and a more fulfilling life.

Gratitude is a powerful tool that can shift one's mindset and attract positivity and abundance into life. When the focus is placed on what there is to be thankful for, it creates space to receive better things. It's a wonderful feeling to recognize what is already present, rather than dwelling on what is missing. That shift in perspective from negative to positive can make a meaningful difference. Still, practicing gratitude can be difficult, especially when life becomes overwhelming.

Many people can relate to feeling stuck in a rut, moving through the motions of daily life without a sense of purpose or fulfillment. There may be financial struggles, strained relationships, or pressure from work or school. In times like these, it's easy to become consumed by negative thoughts and feelings of scarcity. Attention begins to center on what's lacking, rather than what is already there.

In such a mindset, feeling grateful becomes a challenge. It may seem like there's nothing to appreciate, or that things won't improve. Yet gratitude is a choice. It's possible to focus on the good, no matter how small it might be. One can choose to appreciate the people who offer support, the roof over head, or the food on the table.

So why is it so hard to maintain a positive mindset and feel abundant, even when things are tough? One reason is that the human brain is wired to focus on negative thoughts and emotions. This tendency is a leftover from ancient ancestors who needed to be constantly on the lookout for danger to survive. In today's world, however, this negative bias often holds people back from experiencing joy and abundance.

Studies have shown that practicing gratitude can rewire the brain to focus on the positive. It increases feelings of happiness and well-being and can even improve physical health. For example, it has been said that individuals who practice gratitude daily have stronger immune systems and are less likely to get sick — which is something many people have personally experienced, including myself.

I personally believe that gratitude practices can change the way individuals perceive themselves and their lives. By focusing on what they're thankful for, people begin to see themselves as more abundance-minded rather than scarcity-driven. They start to believe there is enough to go around— and that they are worthy of receiving good things. Many have found this shift to be true in their own lives.

Gratitude has the power to transform lives in remarkable ways. One powerful example in my life was a period of hardship when things felt uncertain and overwhelming. During that time, there was a sense of being stuck, unsure of the next steps, and struggling to make ends meet. But through that difficulty, a daily commitment to practicing gratitude made all the difference.

Each morning, I wrote down three things I was thankful for, and I read them out loud to myself before starting my day. At first, routine felt like a chore but, over time, a shift began to happen. Opportunities started to appear where only obstacles had once been seen. Confidence grew. Hope returned. Slowly but steadily, life began to change. The right people showed up. New ideas surfaced. A deep sense of fulfillment began to take root, day by day.

This simple habit—pausing each day to acknowledge gratitude—has the power to shift perspective and create space for abundance. Consider trying it: write down three things to be grateful for. Then observe the feeling it brings. Attracting positivity and abundance starts with gratitude. This simple practice can become a powerful force for change, helping to invite joy, peace, and fulfillment into daily life. Following are eight gratitude writing tips.

1. *Be specific.* Specificity helps foster deeper gratitude. For example, "I'm grateful that my co-workers brought me soup when I was sick on Tuesday" is more impactful than "Grateful for co-workers."

2. *Choose depth over length.* Writing in detail about one meaningful person or moment offers greater benefits than listing many things with little reflection.

3. *Keep it personal.* Focusing on people rather than things tends to create a stronger emotional connection.

4. *Try subtraction, not just addition.* Reflect on what life might look like without certain people or events. This

perspective highlights blessings that may otherwise be overlooked, such as avoided problems or near-misses that turned out well.

5. *See good things as gifts.* Treating positive experiences as gifts encourages appreciation and reduces the tendency to take them for granted.

6. *Savor surprises.* Unexpected events often spark stronger feelings of gratitude. Capture events that were unexpected or surprising, as these tend to elicit stronger levels of gratitude.

7. *Revise repeated entries.* It's okay to write about the same people or things more than once—just explore a new angle or detail each time.

8. *Be consistent.* Whether journaling weekly or every other day, commit to a regular time to journal, then honor that commitment.

Here are more ways to train the brain to practice more gratitude:

Take Time to Notice What's Around You —Practicing mindfulness helps a person tune in to the present moment. Grateful individuals are often more aware of others' gestures. The more frequently one becomes attuned to their surroundings, the greater the chance they'll notice the good around them. This can inspire genuine gratitude, leading to deeper satisfaction and happiness.

The ability to recognize the beauty of nature, small acts of kindness, or the opportunity to earn a living all relies on being aware of oneself and the environment. Whether it's a helping hand in the kitchen or the color of the evening sky, simply noticing these moments creates space for gratitude to grow.

Practice Gratitude for the Little Things—As Jon Kabat-Zinn says, "The little things? The little moments? They aren't little." People often remember to be grateful for big events, like graduating from university or getting married, but it can be more difficult to feel grateful for the small things one does every day.

The simple fact of eating a meal, for example, is special and it can be very powerful. The immediate awareness of the food being presented, combining flavors while satisfying hunger, is a great way to enjoy gratitude often. Another example is feeling grateful in the morning for being able to comfortably sleep at night. People gain comfort, satisfaction, and peace by practicing mindfulness and gratitude in this repeated fashion.

Share Gratitude for Loved Ones—Most people are a little guilty of taking loved ones for granted. The next time a kind act is noticed, why not show gratitude by simply saying "thank you" or offering a hug? Appreciation should be expressed rather than letting kind acts go unnoticed. Training the mind to show gratitude for loved ones can strengthen the relationships with others.

Spread Gratitude via Social Media Platforms—social media can often feel overwhelmingly negative, but it also offers a powerful opportunity to share gratitude and positivity. One way to do this is by posting an uplifting moment from a recent event, a meaningful lesson from a book, or a photo of a place that brings a sense of thankfulness.

Spreading good in a unique and encouraging way helps create a more positive digital atmosphere. This simple act can serve as a reminder that there is still so much to appreciate. Each person has the power to inspire others through this kind of content.

Self-awareness is also essential in the pursuit of happiness. When individuals understand who they are, they begin to make choices that align with their true selves—recognizing their strengths, weaknesses, values, and passions. This clarity allows them to say no to things that drain their energy and yes to what brings joy. The more often they say no to what no longer serves them, the more space they create for what truly matters.

At the core of lasting happiness is a strong sense of self-awareness. It lays the groundwork for meaningful relationships, purposeful careers, and overall well-being. Yet, many people struggle to develop this essential part of themselves. Unlocking it is often the key to discovering true happiness and living a life that feels deeply personal and fulfilling.

One of the main reasons people struggle with self-awareness and happiness is that they're chasing an unrealistic expectation of what happiness should look like. Many get caught up in the social media highlight reels, believing that everyone else has their life together—while they don't. Very few share their struggles, fears, or doubts.

Only by stepping back and recognizing that this experience is shared by many can people begin to break free from unrealistic expectations. Self-awareness and happiness are not impossible goals. They aren't unreachable ideas reserved for a lucky few. With the right mindset and tools, anyone can gain a deeper understanding of themselves and begin living a life that feels truly fulfilling.

So, what is self-awareness? It's the ability to observe thoughts, emotions, and behaviors without judgment. It allows individuals to understand what drives them and what holds them back. Self-awareness helps identify both strengths and limitations, enabling conscious choices that align with personal values and goals. When developed intentionally, it opens the door to a deeper sense of purpose—and a life rich in meaning and fulfillment.

Cultivating self-awareness takes practice. It requires time and effort to develop the habits and skills needed to tune into the inner world. But the payoff is immense. With greater self-awareness, individuals are better equipped to handle challenges, navigate uncertainty and ambiguity, and make choices that align with their true selves.

One of the most powerful moments in my journey of personal growth was when I realized that I had the power to choose how I showed up in the world. I didn't have to be a victim of my circumstances; I could be the architect of my own destiny. It was a moment of profound self-awareness, one that changed the trajectory of my life forever.

Looking back, it becomes clear that self-awareness is a gift that keeps on giving. It unlocks deeper happiness and leads to a life that is authentic, meaningful, and fulfilling. For anyone feeling lost or disconnected, it's important to know there is hope. There is a path forward, 10 Strategies to improve self-awareness—out of the darkness and into the light.

1. Start noticing some reactions. Pay attention to moments when stress, anxiety, or worry arises. Don't judge these feelings try to name them, acknowledge their presence, observe them for a moment, and then let it go.

2. Learn to pause. Take a deep breath in and release it slowly. Bring the focus to the senses. Use the acronym S.T.O.P.: Stop, Take a breath, Observe, Proceed.

Introduce regular mini-resets during the day, where one stays focused for three, five, or ten breaths.

3. Be kind to self, always. Replace self-criticism with acceptance. Practice self-compassion without over-indulging in emotions. As Carl Rogers once said, "Only when I accept myself, just as I am, only then can I begin to change."

4. Get curious. Notice the moods and try to capture some of the thoughts. Write them down. Learn more about oneself through personality assessments, feedback from others, or simply paying better attention in the present moment.

5. Challenge assumptions. People often jump to conclusions without examining them. When individual catches oneself making assumptions, one should ask: Is this true? Is it a fact? Does this thought help or cause harm? Is it useful?

6. Learn not to take things personally. This can be difficult but is essential. What others say or think is usually reflects more about them than about the person receiving it.

7. Be accountable to self and to others. Seek honest feedback. Consider finding an accountability partner—someone who can check in with and is also committed to practicing greater self-awareness. Support and accountability are important on the journey toward deeper awareness.

8. Journal regularly. Getting thoughts out of the head and onto paper can create space between individual

and their emotions. It helps bring perspective and allows for more objective reflection. Clarify priorities, identify what holds one back, and set clear intentions for how to move forward.

9. Live with integrity. Know the core values and act in alignment with them. Be honest both with oneself and with others.

10. Practice meditation and mindfulness. These habits foster calm and clarity, allowing individuals to observe their thoughts in real time. Begin with short, consistent sessions. There will be times when it's challenging. That's part of the lifelong journey. When needed, return to step one and begin again.

Another powerful strategy for finding happiness is mindfulness, a topic that has been talked about throughout this book. Mindfulness means being fully present in the moment, letting go of worries about the past or future, and simply being. It's not always easy, but it's absolutely important. Through mindfulness, the world begins to appear differently. The little things become more visible — the beauty in nature, the kindness of strangers — and that's when the magic begins.

I'll never forget the time I realized I was living someone else's dream, not my own. I was stuck in a job I very much disliked, surrounded by people who didn't support me, and feeling completely lost. But something inside of me clicked. There was a moment of clarity that I had the power to change it. Intentional choices began to emerge, guided by my core values and authentic passions. Saying no to what didn't serve a purpose and yes to what sparked joy became the new way forward in my life. It was truly a liberating experience.

Happiness isn't something that is found. It's something that is created. It's shaped through daily choices, intentional actions, and subtle mindset shifts. It lives in the little things, in small joyful moments that, over time, form a life filled with meaning. Mindfulness practices are helpful ways to create that happiness.

Mindfulness techniques are a powerful way to reduce stress and enhance well-being. These practices help individuals stay grounded in the present moment, acknowledge their feelings, release negative emotions, and cultivate empowering beliefs. With consistent practice, mindfulness can lead to greater emotional self-awareness, mental clarity, and inner peace—while also offering valuable tools for managing stress effectively.

Begin the day with intention. Waking up with intention is a mindful practice that helps set a calm and focused tone for the day ahead. Starting the morning with purpose and awareness can reduce stress and sharpen attention to the present. This might involve taking a few quiet moments to reflect on the goals for the day, while also adjusting one's mindset to face any potential challenges with calmness. Approaching each morning intentionally promotes clarity, peace, and a more positive outlook throughout daily activity.

Pause the autopilot mind. This means becoming aware of thoughts and feelings by taking a step back to observe them without passing judgment or trying to control or alter outcomes. Practicing this technique allows individuals to better accept life's unexpected events and move forward in ways that align with their desired outcomes. Mindfulness exercises like this help build awareness and ownership, leading to positive changes and progress toward personal goals.

Try the five senses exercise. This calming technique helps relax both mind and body by bringing mindful attention to each of the five senses. Begin by sitting comfortably in a quiet space, focusing on the breath for a few minutes. When ready, shift focus to each sense individually: sight, sound, taste, smell, and touch. Take time with each one, simply noticing the experience without judgment or evaluation.

Practice a simple three-step mindfulness routine. This is a helpful introduction to mindfulness for beginners. Start by finding a quiet, comfortable spot to sit without interruption. Focus on breathing, noticing each inhale and exhale. Then, become aware of physical and emotional sensations in the moment. The goal is to observe without judging or attempting to change anything—just noticing and allowing the experience to unfold.

Finally, be grateful for the moment and any insight gained during the exercise. With practice, this simple yet powerful technique can help reduce stress levels while cultivating greater self-awareness and peace of mind leading to a happier and more fulfilled life.

Happiness is achievable. It's not something that happens to a person; it's something one creates through intentional actions and mindset shifts. Choosing to focus on the present, practicing gratitude, and cultivating self-awareness can lead to a life filled with joy and authenticity.

Happiness is living with purpose. It goes beyond achieving dreams. It's about creating a sense of direction and meaning that fuels every action. For many, it means waking up each morning feeling excited and motivated, knowing they're working toward something that truly matters. That's what living a dream life is really about.

It's not always easy. There are still days filled with uncertainty and fear in my life. But the difference now is in how I handle those emotions. They are acknowledged without judgment, and the focus shifts back to the present moment—taking things one step at a time. Self-kindness becomes essential, especially when mistakes happen or expectations aren't met.

When reflecting on my ongoing journey, it became clear that happiness had to be personally defined. For a long time, success and status seemed unattainable. But over time, it became evident that true happiness comes from living in alignment with my personal values and passions. It means waking up with a sense of purpose, feeling confident that progress is being made toward meaningful goals.

There was a pivotal moment in my journey when everything shifted. I was at a crossroads, feeling stuck and unsure of what to do next. And then I realized that I had the power to choose my thoughts, my emotions, and my actions. I had the power to take control of my life and create the reality I wanted. It was a powerful moment, and the impact of that moment remains unforgettable.

Looking back on my journey, it's clear that living a dream-filled, happy, and fulfilled life is truly possible. It requires intention, effort, and the courage to take risks. Most importantly, it demands a strong commitment to personal values and staying true to what matters most.

You've explored what it means to live with meaning — now it's time to embody it. Let this final meditation guide you into presence, gratitude, and the quiet joy that comes when we live fully aligned with who we are.

Conclusion

The journey doesn't begin in some idealized future but right here, right now, in the landscape of the past. The truth is, the power to embrace, evolve, and elevate lies not in escaping yesterday but in understanding it, learning from it, and ultimately making peace with it.

This isn't about dwelling on regrets or romanticizing the so-called good old days. It's about uncovering the buried treasures of experience—both the shining successes and the rough trials—to build a stronger, more resilient, and more fulfilling future.

When the past is seen not as a prison sentence but as a rich tapestry woven with threads of both tears and triumphs, it becomes possible to transform seemingly negative moments—pain, failure, disappointment—into vibrant strands of resilience. These moments strengthen the very fabric of who one becomes. It's not about erasing the past. It's about shifting perspective, uncovering purpose, and recognizing how the past shapes the person is today.

As individuals embrace the lessons etched into the landscape of their lives and allow those lessons to empower them, they become better equipped to navigate future crossroads with confidence, grace, and unwavering self-belief. In doing so, they evolve and create a life rich with presence in each present moment. The power to shape the future lies in the wisdom drawn from the past. Now is the time to unlock that power and elevate life to its fullest potential.

Think of a mighty oak tree. It began as a small, fragile acorn, yet now its roots reach deep into the earth. Storms rage, winds howl, and still, the oak tree stands firm. It doesn't resist the wind — it bends but doesn't break. This is perseverance in action — the quiet strength to adapt and endure. True resilience lies not in unyielding resistance, but in the ability to adjust, to remain grounded, and to thrive despite challenges.

Embracing change isn't about eliminating uncertainty; it's about cultivating the skills and mindset to navigate it gracefully and emerge stronger on the other side. It involves viewing challenges not as obstacles to be overcome, but as opportunities for growth and transformation. It also means being willing to let go of old patterns and beliefs that no longer serve and having the courage to step into the unknown with trust and faith.

It's about developing the flexibility of a willow tree—bending but not breaking in the face of life's storms. It's about trusting in one's own resilience, embracing uncertainty, and believing in the capacity to adapt and thrive, no matter what life brings. The journey of self-mastery is a continuous process of learning and evolution, a testament to the human capacity for growth and transformation.

The profound impact of personal growth lies in embracing the past, evolving into one's best self, and elevating life to new heights. But true elevation isn't a solitary climb. It is a shared ascent—a collective journey where individuals reach back to help others climb alongside them. This is the essence of leaving a legacy: not just the mark left on the world, but the positive ripple effect created through intentional actions and the mentorship of others.

Elevating life to the next level means building a legacy that extends beyond a single lifetime. A legacy isn't built on one act; it is constructed brick by brick, decision by decision, action by action, over the course of a life lived with intention. It is about weaving a tapestry of positive impact—threads of kindness, generosity, and wisdom interwoven to create a vibrant and enduring pattern.

The journey toward inner peace, the cornerstone of a fulfilling life, is not a sprint to a finish line but a lifelong pilgrimage. It is a continuous unfolding, a process of constant refinement and growth, much like a river carving its path through the landscape. There will be moments of calm, reflecting the tranquil pools along the river's course, and moments of turbulence, like rapids and waterfalls that inevitably arise. The key is not to avoid the turbulent stretches but to navigate them with grace and awareness, recognizing that these challenges are essential parts of the journey.

Embrace the ebb and flow of life. Accept that periods of peace and tranquility will be interspersed with times of stress, uncertainty, and even suffering. These difficult experiences are not barriers; they are valuable teachers, offering opportunities for growth and self-discovery. Each challenge faced and each obstacle overcome builds resilience and deepens one's understanding of self and the world. Rather than striving for a life free of hardship, aim to cultivate a mindset capable of navigating life's complexities with wisdom, compassion, and composure.

There will be triumphs to celebrate and setbacks to overcome. The key is to maintain a balanced perspective—acknowledging both the highs and the lows, celebrating the successes, and learning from the setbacks. Embrace the journey, appreciate the process, and celebrate the progress. The view from the summit will be all the more breathtaking because of it.

Life is not a straight path—it is a sacred rhythm of rising and falling, of breaking and becoming. Seasons of stillness will meet moments of stretching. Periods of comfort will give way to deep calls for growth. But within every trial, there is a treasure. Within every setback, there is a setup for something greater. The struggles are not punishments—they are passages, invitations to awaken, expand, and rise.

Do not fear the valleys or resist the storms. They are not here to break; they are here to build. Each experience—joyful or painful—carries divine purpose. Let the heart remain open. Let the spirit remain teachable. Let the soul remain anchored in truth. This is the journey of transformation. This is the path of healing.

As you embrace the past, you release its hold.

As you evolve in the present, you align with purpose.

As you elevate into the future, you become all you were created to be.

You Are Unforgettable.

You Are Unstoppable.

You Are Undeniably Divine in Purpose.

Now is the time to rise. To breathe. To believe. To begin again. To embrace and let it go. To evolve and let it be. To elevate and let it come.

Healing is not just in the reading—it's in the stillness that follows. As you listen to the meditation, open your heart, align your energy, and welcome the Divine guidance that is always with you. Your transformation begins now.

About the Author

Kobi Julian is a transformational life coach, motivational speaker, and the inspiring author behind *Embrace Evolve Elevate*. With a master's degree in health and another in education, Kobi has been a wellness and fitness business owner for 16 years. She brings a unique blend of personal experience, professional insight, and spiritual wisdom to every message she shares.

Born into a Muslim family and raised in a culture that often suppressed the individual voice, Kobi's life journey is one of resilience, reinvention, and redemption. From fleeing war and personal loss to finding her voice and faith in a new land, she has walked through pain and emerged with purpose. Her lived experiences fuel her deep passion to help women break free from the pain of their past, embrace their true identity, and rise into lives of meaning, peace, and power.

Whether coaching, teaching, or writing, Kobi's mission is clear: to help others build their courage so they can find purpose through their pain. Her book, *Embrace Evolve Elevate* is a reflection of that mission—a guide to transformation that is both deeply personal and universally empowering.